D0072295

Centre Formation, Protest Movements, and Class Structure in Europe and the United States

S. N. Eisenstadt, L. Roniger, and A. Seligman

New York University Press, New York

Manufactured in Great Britain

First published in the USA in 1987 by
NEW YORK UNIVERSITY PRESS,
Washington Square, New York, N.Y. 10003

Library of Congress Cataloging-in-Publication Data

Eisenstadt, S. N. (Shmuel Noah), 1923–
  Centre formation, protest movements, and class
structure in Europe and the United States.

  Includes bibliographies and index.
  1. Political sociology.   2. Elite (Social sciences)
3. Political participation.   4. Social change.
5. Comparative government.   I. Roniger, L. (Luis),
1949–   .   II. Seligman A.   III. Title.
JA76.E57   1987   306'.2'091821   86-31300
ISBN 0-8147-2171-0

Contents

List of contributors

S. N. Eisenstadt is Professor of Sociology at the Hebrew University of Jerusalem, where he has been a faculty member since 1946. He has served as a Visiting Professor at Harvard, M.I.T., Chicago, Michigan, Oslo, Zurich and Vienna. His publications include *From Generation to Generation* (Free Press, 1956), *The Political System of Empires* (Free Press, 1963), *Israeli Society* (Basic Books, 1968), *Tradition, Change and Modernity* (Basic Books, 1973), *The Form of Sociology*, with M. Curelaru (John Wiley, 1976), *Patrons, Clients and Friends*, with L. Roniger (Cambridge University Press, 1984), *The Transformation of Israeli Society* (Weidenfeld & Nicholson, 1985), and *Society, Culture and Urbanization*, with A. Schachar (Sage Publications, 1985).

Luis Roniger is a member of the Departments of Sociology and Social Anthropology, and Spanish and Latin American Studies of the Hebrew University. He has researched and published in the fields of interpersonal relations and the comparative study of clientelism. His forthcoming book on *Hierarchy and Trust in Modern Mexico and Brazil* will be published by the University of New Mexico Press.

Adam Seligman teaches in the Department of Sociology and Social Anthropology of the Hebrew University. At present he is completing a study on *Human Agency, The Millennium and Social Change* in seventeenth century New England. His major research interests are in the fields of historical sociology and social theory.

With a chapter contributed by

Sarah Levinthal who is a doctoral student at the University of Toronto, and researcher associated with the Ontario Retail Council (CLC–AFL–CIO). Her major research interest is in labor relations.

Introduction

The various essays brought together in this book are based on an approach to the analysis of political processes that has been developed in a series of studies at the Department of Sociology and the Truman Research Institute of the Hebrew University. It can be called the 'civilisational approach', and it is based on the major assumption that it is not possible to understand fully many central aspects of political process by taking the definition of the state and of political institutions, for granted; or, by defining the state or political institutions solely in terms of political power and of the activities of different political and administrative agents, and by their relative strength *vis-à-vis* other groups, especially classes or various interest groups within a society.

In addition to these variables or aspects of the political process—the importance of which nobody can deny—it is of central importance to analyse the social context of political institutions, and in particular the symbolic meanings which people attribute to these institutions, beyond their formal definition. Thus, the sources and criteria of evaluation of political institutions as they develop and necessarily change, in the broader context and historical experience of human civilisations, must be opened to sociological inquiry.

Of special importance in this context are the ways in which such experience shapes certain underlying premises of the political realm. Among such premises are certain assumptions of authority, justice and the place of political activity in the overall conception of human action. It is our claim that such premises and their embodiment in the institutional structure of society are effected through the activities of the major social elites and in particular, the political ones. Through the interaction of these elites the various forms of social control are ordered and challenges to this control, articulated. The activities of these elites are not however limited to the exercise of power in a specific political sense. They may indeed represent class interests. Yet our own inquiry will attempt to reveal to what extent these elites, when articulating class-related demands and protest, do so in a way that is specifically informed by their overall set of value assumptions and premises.

The studies brought together in this book attempt to apply this civilisational approach to the analysis of centre formation and protest in modern Europe and the United States. The major working hypothesis of these studies has been that the crystallisation of the modern state in general and the nation-state in particular in the post-Reformation period and throughout the eighteenth and nineteenth centuries in Europe and later the United States, Australia and Canada represents a unique development in the structuring of centre–periphery relations.

The starting point of these studies has been the fact that most modern European and American centres have been constituted through a revolutionary process so that symbols of protest in general and of class protest in particular have been incorporated into the centres of most of these countries. Thus movements of protest in general and of class struggle in particular could become legitimate as central aspects of their demands were incorporated into the centre. It is a closely related fact that one of the specific characteristics of European civilisation has been the continuous confrontation between centre and periphery. This confrontation has often resulted in the periphery attaining some measure of autonomy from the centre, or through its impingement on the centre, influencing and even transforming it.

Even within Europe and America such a development has however, not been even. Great differences have existed within these Western societies. In Northern Europe, for instance, protest seemed to have been incorporated as a legitimate facet of socio-political life. By contrast, in Mediterranean settings, protest was often rejected, eliciting responses that did not enhance the viability of political institutions. Differences of course existed also within the different nation-states in each geopolitical area. As a result these Western societies present an ideal setting for controlled comparative studies.

The studies in this volume seek to relate these characteristics of centre–periphery relations in Europe, and in the United States, to two major axes of analysis. The first axis concerns the cultural orientations pertaining to basic aspects of social order, such as the nature of the relation between the transcendental and mundane orders, the degree of autonomy between them, of dissociation and mutual relevance, and primarily the types of activities emphasised as crucial to bridging the chasm between the transcendental and mundane spheres.

The second axis focuses on the roles played by social, political and cultural elites who articulated and reformulated these conceptions within the different Western societies. It was through their relations with each other and with the social centre, that the major contours of different societies crystallised in specific ways. In this context, the character of social stratification, of protest articulation and the modes of its incorporation into the centre, constituted crucial factors in connecting the realms of cultural orientations and institutional structures with the process of socio-cultural and political restructuring, within the different societies.

Accordingly, we analyse the core cultural orientations predominant in Western European and American civilization. These are related to the construction of Western-European and American centres through the activities of various elites, counter-elites and protest movements. In these studies major differences between various Western societies are indicated. Specifically, the analyses of France, Italy, Spain, England and the United States, explore, along historical lines and from a sociological perspective, aspects of unity and divergence in the constitution of a modern socio-political order.

The essays in the first section of this volume are devoted to the main political aspects of this process—the different forms of political participation, the construction of national centres and the impingement of protest on these centres. The second section of the volume is devoted to the study of the structural aspects of the modern social order, focusing on the analysis of social stratification, and the formation of diverse types of social hierarchies in Southern Europe and in America. In particular we analyse the complex inter-weaving of social (class) identities and modes of political action in these societies.

The research on which these studies are based has been supported by a generous grant from the Volkswagen Foundation. The final stages of this research and especially the work on France were aided by a grant from La Fondation Joseph Nahmias créér sous l'egide de la Fondation Genérale Pierre Koenig. Thanks are due as well to Ms. Edna Sachar for her editorial assistance and to Morissa Amittai and Naomi Miller for the final preparation of the book.

S. N. Eisenstadt
L. Roniger
A. Seligman
Jerusalem
July, 1986

Part I: Centres and protest in Europe and the United States

1 Centre formation and protest movements in Europe and the United States: a comparative perspective

S. N. Eisenstadt

Basic assumptions of the civilisational approach

In this chapter I would like first to spell out, in somewhat greater detail, the basic assumptions of the sociological approach to comparative civilisations and then apply it to the European and American scene, and to the concrete themes developed in this collection of essays.

The crux of this approach is that the analysis of the formation and dynamics of institutional settings of different societies has to take into account the basic premises of civilisations and their implications on those processes through which social action is structured and a perduring normative order is established. At the same time it is clear that no institutional formation, no system or pattern of social interaction—whether micro- or macro-sociological—is or can be stable. The very processes of control—symbolic and organisational alike—through which such patterns are formed, generate also tendencies to protest, conflict and change. Because every social order contains a strong element of dissent regarding the distribution of power and the values upheld, no institutional system is ever fully 'homogeneous,' in the sense of being accepted either fully or to the same degree by all of those participating in it.

Even if, for very long periods of time, a great majority of the members of a given society identify to some degree with the values and norms of a given system and are willing to provide it with the resources it needs, other tendencies develop which may give rise to change in the attitudes of social groups to the basic premises of the institutional system.

Thus, in any society, there exists the possibility that 'anti-systems' may develop within it. While anti-systems often remain latent for long periods of time, under propitious conditions they may also constitute important foci of systemic change. That such potential anti-systems exist in all societies is evinced by the potential existence in all of them of themes and orientations of protest, as well as of social movements and cultural and religious heterodoxies.

Such latent anti-systems may be activated and lead to far reaching changes by the very processes connected with the continuity and maintenance, or reproduction, of different settings of social interaction in general, and of the macro-societal order in particular. The most important of these processes are: (1) shifts in the relative power positions and aspirations of different categories and groups; (2) the activation in the younger generation, particularly in those who belong to the upper classes and the elites, of the potential rebelliousness and antinomian orientations inherent in the very act of socialisation; (3) several socio-morphological or socio-demographic processes through which the biological reproduction of populations is connected with the social reproduction of settings of social interaction; and (4) the interaction between such settings and their natural and intersocietal environments, for example, movements of population or conquest.

The crystallisation of these potentialities of change usually takes place through the activities of secondary elites who attempt to mobilise various groups and resources in order to change aspects of the social order as it was shaped by the coalition of ruling elites. Thus, though every civilisation or social system constructs some specific systemic boundaries within which it operates, the very construction of such civilisational or social systems also generates conflict and contradictions which may lead to transformation or decline; that is, to different modes of restructuring their boundaries. As a result there always exists the possibility that the integrative and regulative mechanisms inherent in any society may fail.

While these potentialities for conflict and change are inherent in all human societies, their concrete development—their intensity and the concrete directions of change and transformation they engender—vary greatly between different societies and civilisations. They differ according to the different constellations of cultural orientations and social factors, i.e., elites, patterns of the social division of labour and political–ecological settings and processes. These constellations shape the different patterns of social conflict, social movements, rebellions and heterodoxy that develop in different societies, as well as the relation of these movements to processes of institution building. They shape the direction of institutional change, the degree to which changes in different aspects of the institutional order coalesce and their consequent transformation patterns.

The Axial Age Civilisations

The comparative approach to the study of civilisations has been developed in Jerusalem in terms of analyses of comparative civilisations in general and of so-called Axial Age Civilisations in particular[1], of which the Christian and European ones constitute crucial and distinctive cases.

The term Axial Age Civilisations was used by Karl Jaspers to describe those (Great) civilizations which developed in the first millenium before the Christian era—namely Ancient Israel, later on Christianity in its great variety, Ancient Greece, Ancient China in the early Imperial period, Hinduism and Buddhism, and much later, beyond the Axial Age proper, Islam.[2] The specific, distinctive characteristics of these civilisations was the development and institutionalisation within them in general, and within their centres in particular, of basic conceptions of tension, of a chasm between the transcendental and mundane order.

These conceptions of a basic tension between the transcendental and the mundane order have developed above all among small groups of 'intellectuals' which constituted a new social element, a new type of elite in general and carriers of models of cultural and social order in particular. But ultimately these conceptions were, in all these Axial Age civilisations, institutionalised, that is, became the predominant orientation of both the ruling as well as of many secondary elites, fully embodied in their respective centres or subcentres, transforming the nature of the political elites and making the intellectuals into relatively autonomous partners in the central coalitions. Thus the various disperse groups of intellectuals became transformed into more fully crystallised and institutionalised ones, often into clerics—be it the Jewish Prophets and Priests, the Great Greek Philosophers, the Chinese Literati, the Hindu Brahmins, the Buddhist Sangha or the Islamic Ulama. The most important repercussions of such institutionalisation has been the development of ideological and structural attempts to reconstruct the mundane world according to the basic conception of resolution of this tension. The given mundane order was perceived in these civilisations as incomplete, often as faulty and in need of being reconstructed, at least in some of its parts, according to the conception of the resolution of this basic tension, or, to use Weberian nomenclature, according to the premises of salvation—basically a Christian term, the equivalents of which can however be found in other civilisations.

As part of this process took place, in all these civilisations a far–reaching restructuring of the conception of the relation between the political and the higher, transcendental order. The political order, as the central focus or framework of mundane order has been in these civilisations usually conceived as lower than the transcendental one and accordingly had to be restructured according to the premises of the latter. It was the rulers who were usually held to be responsible for assuming such structuring of the political order; and accordingly there appeared the possibility of calling a ruler to judgment in the name of some higher order, to which the rulers were accountable.

At the same time the nature of the rulers became greatly transformed. The King–God, the embodiment of the cosmic and earthly order alike, disappeared, and a secular ruler, in principle accountable to some higher order appeared. Thus there emerged the conception of the accountability of the rulers and often of the community as well to a higher authority—God, Divine Law and the like. Accordingly, the possibility of calling a ruler to judgment emerged. The first most dramatic appearance of this conception took place in Ancient Israel, in the priestly and prophetic pronounciations. A different conception of such accountability, an accountability of the community and its laws, appeared on the northern shores of the Eastern Mediterranean, in Ancient Greece. In different forms a conception of accountability appeared in all these civilisations.

Concomitant to the emergence of conceptions of accountability there began to develop autonomous spheres of law and conceptions of rights, as distinct from ascriptively bound customs. Closely related to these changes in the basic political conceptions there developed far-reaching transformations of the conceptions of personal identity.

The interpersonal virtues such as solidarity, mutual help or the like, were taken out of their primordial framework and combined, in different dialectical modes, with the attributes of resolution of the tension between the transcendental and the mundane orders. In this way they generated a new level of internal tensions in the structuring of personality, and it was through the appropriate reconstruction of personality that the bridging of the tension between the transcendental and the mundane order, i.e. salvation, could be attained. This was closely connected with the development of conceptions of the individual as an independent autonomous entity, very often out of tune with the political order. Both European and non-European Axial civilizations share this combination of the idea of accountability with a conception of the individual personality.

But the nature of these conceptions and of their ideological and institutional implications varied greatly between the European and the other civilisations, as well as to some degree, within Europe. For instance they differed in the specific definitions of the tension between the transcendental and mundane order and in the ways to overcome it that became predominant in these civilisations and societies, in their basic premises of relations between state and society, and in their conceptions of authority, hierarchy and equality.

In the following pages we shall analyse some of the distinctive characteristics of European civilisations in the framework of Axial Age civilisations in general and of their respective patterns of modernity in particular.

The specific characteristics of European civilisation

European civilisation has developed some distinctive characteristics within the broad framework of the Axial Age Civilisations. It was characterised by a very high degree of multiplicity and cross-cutting of cultural orientations and structural settings. The symbolic pluralism of heterogeneity of European society was evident in the multiplicity of traditions out of which its own cultural tradition crystallised—the Judeo-Christian, the Greek, the Roman and the various tribal ones, and unlike the case of Islam, by a great multiplicity of cultural codes and orientations.[3] Most important among these orientations or codes was the emphasis on a high autonomy of the cosmic, cultural and social orders and a high level of mutual relevance between them which was defined in terms of the tension between the transcendental and the mundane order; the multiplicity and complexity of the different ways of resolving this tension, either through worldly (political and economic) or 'other-worldly' activities.

The second cultural orientation prevalent in European civilisation was a high level of activism and commitment of broader groups and strata to these orders. Third, was the conception of a high degree of relatively autonomous access of different groups and strata to these orders—to some degree countered by, and in constant tension with, the strong emphasis on the mediation of access by such bodies as the Church or the political powers. Fourth, was the definition of the individual as an autonomous and responsible entity with respect to access to these orders.

This multiplicity of symbolic orientations became connected with a very special type of structural–organisational pluralism in Europe.[4] This type of pluralism differed greatly from the one that developed, for instance, in the Byzantine Empire which shared many aspects of its cultural traditional models with Western Europe. Within the Byzantine

Empire this pluralism was manifest in a relatively high degree of structural differentiation within a rather unified socio-political framework in which different social functions were apportioned to different groups and social categories. The structural pluralism that developed in Europe was characterised, above all, by a strong combination between low, but continuously increasing, levels of structural differentiation on the one hand, and continuously changing boundaries of different collectivities, units and frameworks on the other.

Between these collectivities and units there did not exist a clear cut division of labour. Rather there tended to develop among them a continuous competition over their respective standing with respect to the different attributes of social and cultural order; over the performance of the major societal functions—be they economic, political or cultural—as well as over the very definition of the boundaries of ascriptive communities.

The combination of these symbolic models and structural conditions generated several basic institutional characteristics particularly in structure of centres and the relation to the periphery, which developed with great variations in medieval and early modern times in Western and Central Europe. These characteristics were an interesting mixture of Imperial and 'real' feudal institutions, as distinct from a simple decentralisation or disintegration of large patrimonial or tribal units. These feudal institutions shared several crucial characteristics with Imperial societies, probably because they emerged from within civilisations with an Imperial past and aspirations as Otto Hintze has shown long ago.[5] The most important of these aspirations was the symbolic and to some degree the organisational distinctiveness of the centre. But unlike purely Imperial societies, the most outstanding characteristic of the structure of the centres in feudal societies is that there existed within them many centres and subcentres, all of which tended to have multiple orientations—political, cultural and economic. These centres and subcentres tended to become arranged in a rather complicated but never in a unified, rigid hierarchy in which none of them was clearly predominant. Naturally enough, the activities of the dominant centres were of a wider scope than those of the local ones, but even these centres did not have a total monopoly on social resources and mechanisms of institutional control. Each of the local centres had some degree of independent dominance over some of its resources, over the mobilisation of its activities, as well as over its access to the dominant centres.

Moreover, these various centres were not completely separated from one another. There existed continuous mutual orientations, as well as structural interrelations among them. In addition, any group with control over some resources necessary for the development of the political or cultural orientation of the centres had some legitimate and autonomous, even if differentiated, access to such centres. Not only the Church, but also many local or status groups were to some degree autonomous in their ability to convert their resources from one institutional sphere to another and from the periphery to the centres.[6]

In close relation with these orientations the societies of Western Europe have also been continuously characterised by a high degree of commitment by centres and periphery alike to common 'ideals' and goals. Both the traditional—the absolutist and 'estate'—rulers of Western Europe (and, as we shall see later on, the leaders of modern 'nation-states' or class societies) have laid special emphasis on the development of common symbols of cultural and political goals, as well as on a high degree of regulation of the relations among different, relatively independent, groups.

Patterns of centre and strata formation and of institution-building in Europe

In a parallel manner there developed in Europe several specific characteristics of centre and strata formation, as listed below.

First, the multiplicity of centres in European Societies prevented the development of a closed (caste-like) occupational system, despite the strong tendencies in that direction. Every major autonomous social unit—the church, the court, and various social strata—tended to develop a different scale of evaluation, each with a logical claim of general validity. As a result, a multiplicity of status hierarchies tended to develop. Persons who ranked high in one hierarchy might rank low in another, and vice versa—a phenomenon that sociologists have labelled status incongruency. Thus another result was a gradual blurring of the distinction between free and servile groups.

Second, there was a strong tendency toward a relatively unified class consciousness and class organisation. This was especially evident among the higher strata, but was also found among the middle and even the lower free strata. The fullest expression of this tendency is found in the system of presentation that culminated in the form of estates and parliaments, the roots of which were in the tradition of political participation in the centre available to most groups simply by virtue of their identities as corporate or semicorporate bodies. In sharp contrast to the situation in other societies such as China, countrywide class consciousness and organisation were not confined to the higher status groups, they could also be found among the middle and even the lowest free groups and strata.

Third, unlike Russia and China, but not entirely unlike India, Western and Central Europe tended to develop a close relationship between family and kinship identity on the one hand and class identity on the other. Family and kinship groups were very important agencies, not only for orienting their members toward the attainment of high positions, but also for transmitting these positions to them by ascription. In Western and Central Europe, however, there was a good deal of open conflict over the degree to which each stratum should participate in the centre. Theoretically, at least, this could not happen in India where the levels of differential participation were fixed by ritualistic ascription (although the practice was subject to exceptions).[7]

Fourth, each social stratum, especially the middle ones, tended to encompass a great variety of occupational positions and organisations and link them in a way of life with a common avenue to access to the centre. In this, Europe again resembled India, more than Russia or China.[8]

Fifth, closely related to the four preceding characteristics was the possibility of differential yet common participation in various cultural orders and centres by different groups and strata. This, in turn, made the life styles of different strata overlap. Thus the availability of several channels of access to the same centre—channels that could be used by various social strata—made contact between the strata much easier.[9]

Sixth, with respect to social mobility, we find a high degree of family mobility among strata at all levels of society. This had its roots, as Marc Bloch has indicated, in the feudal period,[10] and it seems to have continued up to the end (or at least the middle) of the absolutist era. Thus the fact that Europe's social strata had a collective consciousness and organisation that embraced the whole society facilitated continuous changes in the family and ethnic composition of various groups. This mobility was, on the whole, more of the so-called contested, than of a sponsored type, although the latter was also present. In sharp contrast to China, but in some ways like India (with its process of subcaste formation), European society developed not only a process of mobility within a relatively fixed system of positions but a process that, in itself, created new positions and status systems. The most obvious illustration of this phenomenon is the development of cities, which occurred, of course, long before the age of absolutism. In the late medieval city especially, new points of contact arose between different groups and strata, serving as foci for the development of new forms of political and social consciousness.[11]

Thus the pattern of class struggle and consciousness that developed in Europe from the late Middle Ages and continuing into the modern era, was based on several assumptions or premises, the most important of which were: (a) a tendency to autonomous access of major groups to those social and cultural attributes which serve as bases of the criteria of status, as well as of autonomous access to the centres of the society; (b) a high degree of status association and perception of common class interests among relatively diversified occupational groups; (c) a relatively high degree of country-wide strata or class consciousness which tends to minimise, from the point of view of strata formation, the importance of ethnic, religious or regional groups, and which are characterised by (d) a high degree of political articulation and expression of their respective class interests and conflicts; (e) continuous attempts by different strata to acquire access to the centre or centres, to participate in them and to change them, and above all to minimise the principles of hierarchy as against those of equality in access to them.

All these tendencies and orientations were based on the assumption, to a very large degree unique to European civilisation, that economic power can be converted directly, not only into prestige, but also into political power without losing its autonomous standing and legitimation.

The preceding analysis indicates that the full crystallisation of the structural tendencies, combined with the specific cultural orientations prevalent in Europe, gave rise there to (a) multiplicity of centres; (b) a high degree of permeation of the peripheries by the centres and of impingement of the peripheries on the centres; (c) a relatively small degree of overlapping of the boundaries of class, ethnic, religious and political entities and their continuous restructuring; (d) a comparatively high degree of autonomy of groups and strata and of their access to the centres of society; (e) a high degree of overlapping among different status units combined with a high level of countrywide status ('class') consciousness and political activity; (f) multiplicity of cultural and 'functional' (economic, or professional) elites with a relatively high degree of autonomy, a high degree of cross-cutting between them and close relationships between them and broader, more ascriptive strata; (g) a relative autonomy of the legal system with regard to other integrative systems, above all the political and religious ones; and (h) a high degree of autonomy of cities and autonomous centres of social and structural creativity and identity-formation.

Patterns of protest and change in European civilisation

In close relation to these institutional features of 'traditional' European civilisation there developed within it a special pattern of change. This pattern of change was characterised by a relatively high degree of articulation of political struggle and symbolic and ideological structuring of movements of protest, as well as by a high degree of coalescence of change and the restructuring of political regimes and other components of the macro-societal order.

Thus changes within any component of the macro-societal order impinged on one another and above all on the political sphere. These changes gave rise to a continuous process of social restructuring. As compared with the pure Imperial systems, Western Europe was characterised by much less stability of regimes, by continuous changes of boundaries of collectivities and restructuring of centres, but at the same time it evinced also a much greater capacity of institutional innovation cutting across different political and 'national' boundaries and centres.

These changes were activated by: (a) secondary elites, relatively close to the centre, highly predisposed to be the major carrier of religious heterodoxies and political innovations; (b) a relatively close relationship between these autonomous secondary elites and broader social strata; (c) a concomitant predisposition on the part of these elites and broader social strata to develop activities oriented to centre formation and to combine them with those of institution-building in the economic, cultural and educational spheres.

Out of these tendencies there developed a continuous confrontation between the construction of centres and the processes of institution-building. Institution-building in most spheres was seen as very relevant to the construction of centres and judged according to its contribution to their basic premises. At the same time centres were judged according to their capacity to promote just and meaningful institutions, and as such, were subject to the continuous competition on the part of different groups and elites over the terms of access to these centres and the definition thereof.[12]

The impact of Protestantism—the revolutionary origins of European modernity and the characteristics of protest orientations in modern Europe–the tension between state and society

It was within the framework of these broad cultural orientations and structural features that the specific 'mutation', the heterodoxy of

Protestantism, could develop and perhaps above all to have the varied symbolic and institutional impacts which Max Weber and later scholars attributed to it.[13] The most forceful of these impacts could be perhaps discerned in the revolutionary origins and breakthroughs of European modernity, in the Great Revolutions—the English, American, French, and later on the Russian, which in their turn have generated the specific patterns of modern protest orientations and of their incorporation into the centres in Europe.

The focus of the modern European order has been, as often stressed in sociological literature, that the exploration of continuously expanding human and natural environments and their mastery could be attained by the conscious effort of man in society. The fullest expression of this attitude could be found in the breakthrough of science, that is, in the premises that the exploration of nature by man is an 'open' enterprise which creates a new cultural order; that the continuous expansion of scientific and technological knowledge could transform both the cultural and social orders and create new, external and internal environments to be endlessly explored by man, but at the same time, harnessed to both his intellectual vision and technical needs.[14] Science and technological knowledge were only one aspect of European modernity. Other aspects entailed the formation of a 'rational' culture, an efficient economy, a civil (class) society and nation-states where these tendencies of 'rational' expansion could become fully articulated, and which would also create a social and political order based on freedom.

Thus the new civilisation of modernity, which emerged from this background was based ideologically and politically on the assumption of equality and of growing participation of the citizens in the centre. This was most clearly manifest in the tendency to establish universal citizenship and suffrage and some semblance of a 'participant' political or social order, giving rise to ideologies of participation.

It was out of these orientations that some of the specific assumptions about patterns of participation and protest characteristics of the modern European societies and nation-states developed leading ultimately, but only ultimately, to the potentialities of *Entzauberung*.[15] The most important of these assumptions were: first, that the major social and political forces (the political elites as well as the state) on the one hand, and 'society' on the other, continuously struggled about their relative importance in the formation and crystallisation of the cultural and political centres of the nation-state and the regulation of access to it, and about the access to the transcendental attributes which these centres represented; second was the assumption that the processes of structural change and dislocation, which developed as a result of the processes of modernisation, gave rise not only to various concrete problems and demands, but also the growing quest for participation in the broader social and political orders. This quest for participation of the periphery in such social, political and cultural orders was mostly manifest in the search for access to these centres.

These assumptions about the nature of participation in the centre were connected with specific types of orientations to protest that developed in European societies. These orientations to protest provided the concrete contents of the quest for such participation.

The first basic theme of protest focused on the search for principles of social order and justice, and for the legitimation of the centre in general and of the ruling groups in particular in terms of some non-traditional values, acceptable to broader strata, and to some extent, shared and even 'created' by them.

The second theme focused on the nature of the emerging overall civil, political and cultural community, especially on the finding of new common symbols in which various groups of society could find some sense of personal and collective identity.

The third major theme of protest focused around the possibility of attaining full expression of human and cultural creativity, of personal dignity, and of true or pure interpersonal relations with the specialised and differentiated frameworks attendant on modernisation and the complex division of labour involved. Basic to this theme was the problem of alienation, that is, of the assumed loss by individuals of the direct relation to and identification with their work, their social setting, and other people.

Around these focal themes of protest there developed different principled orientations which in reality often tended to overlap. One such orientation, usually called the 'rightist' one, was rooted in the continuous feeling by different groups of being ousted and deposed from existing positions and values, of losing their place in the society, and the consequent development by them of demands for upholding and/or restoring traditional order and values. Another, what may be called the 'leftist' orientation, was aimed at effecting far-reaching changes in the social structure, in the basic principles of allocation which would favour those groups or classes which allegedly were formerly deprived of advantageous positions, or full participation. These groups could be social 'classes,' occupational categories, regional groups within any certain society, or special overall national or tribal subgroups within a broad (Imperial, colonial or international) social and political order.

Both these orientations became interrelated in different ways with the search for direct, 'pure', unalienated human relations and attachments to primordial symbols. Traditionalists would claim that such relations are possible only under relatively stable, ordered conditions, undiluted by the disrupting forces of growing differentiation, 'democratisation' and mass society. Political 'radicals,' on the other hand, would claim that such relations could be achieved only by overthrowing such order and establishing a new one whose institutional arrangements would entirely coalesce with 'nonalienated' relations. Other more 'non-political' radicals would claim that such relations could be attained only outside the political realm.

The history of modern European social and political movements can be, at least, on the ideological level, depicted in terms of these varied ideological orientations and their constellations, and it was in terms of such orientations that modern societies responded to the various crises which developed within them. Whatever the differences between the ideological constellations that developed in Europe, all these movements combined an emphasis on some orientation to the transcendental realm and of relating such orientations to socio-political realities, with the struggle to define the relative importance of social and political groups as carriers of such orientations.

In the earlier stages of European modernity it was assumed that through the reorganisation of the political-national centres, most social problems, especially the problems of meaningful participation in socio-cultural orders on the one hand, and the problems generated by industrialisation on the other, would be solved.

Social-political centres were viewed as the major foci and frameworks of charismatic orientations through which the modern social and cultural orders were defined, and also as the major reference points of individuals' cultural and collective identity. They were also conceived as being able, through a series of appropriate social policies or through revolutionary changes, to restructure those aspects of modern economy which were felt to be most conducive to alienation and anomie. Thus, in the first stages of modernity, most movements of social protest revolved around the broadening of the scope of participation and channels of access to the centres, changing or reforming their cultural and social contents, solving the problems of unequal participation in them, and finding ways to attenuate or overcome, through the policies of the centre.

These movements of protest have crystallised around two foci —those of the nation-state and those of class society. The former epitomised the crystallisation of the new types of collectivities and centres that developed in modern Europe; the latter, concerns the mode of structuring class-consciousness and activities, and the relations between 'State' and 'Society'. The second point, perhaps seen best in the socialist movements, has constituted a continuation, in conditions of modernity, of the patterns of class-formation that have developed in Europe.

The formation of these new centres and the movements of protest attendant to them was not, of course, a smooth process; it was a process of continuous struggle and was full of crises, the nature of which cannot be fully understood without recourse to basic premises of European civilisation.

Differences within Western Europe and the United States

Needless to say, there developed within Europe far-reaching differences in the concrete crystallisation of the above premises, as the essays collected in this book fully attest to. The major distinction within Europe was that between the concrete structuring of class consciousness and protest and the relative centrality of those protest movements in the construction of the centres. The degree to which a symbolism of protest was incorporated into them, and the degree to which viable nation-state centres were constructed early in the history of modern states, has also to be taken into account.

These variations were indeed connected with the structure of elites and especially the degree of their autonomy, the major cultural orientations articulated by such elites, and the major types of coalitions between different elites. Some of the major (often cross-cutting) distinctions have been those between Northern and Southern Europe, between Protestant and Catholic countries, and between states with a long history of unity as against more recent ones. There is also a strong, although not universal, tendency to overlap between these two categories.

These differences in class formation, protest movements and crystallisation of elites, were also very closely related to the nature of the structure of patron-client relations in different European societies. Thus, it is well known that in the Mediterranean societies—Spain, Portugal, Italy and Greece—patron-client relations, whether in the form of traditional patron-client relations or in the form of more modern parties, or bureaucratic and administrative networks, constituted not only, as in other European countries, important addenda to the central core of their institutional structure, but indeed made up the very core of this structure.[16] Whatever the differences between different European societies, they all shared a continuous tension between direct and indirect access to the centre, as well as between principles of hierarchy and equality, as basic symbolic components of their respective societies.

All these basic ideological premises—and their impact on the structure of centres, on the very conception of the political realm, and the composition of elites—were totally transformed in North America, first in the Puritan colonies, and after the American revolution, in the United States as a whole. This transformation was expressed in the strong emphasis developed in the United States on the metaphysical equality of all members of the community, so firmly stressed by Alexis de Tocqueville, on the unmediated access of all members of the community to the centre and on the almost total denial of the symbolic validity of hierarchy as a basic component of these premises.[17]

Of basic importance to these characteristics of the United States was the fact that access to the centre was given, in principle, to all citizens. In close relation to the conceptions of equality mentioned above, access to the centre did not constitute, as in Europe, a focus of principled struggle. Concomitantly, the confrontation between state and society typically found in Europe was less prominent, with society in some way submerging the state within itself. As a result concepts and ideologies of the 'state' (as distinct from the 'republic' or the 'people') did not develop.

Another important factor in this development was the structure of elites and of the specific formation of strata that took place in the United States. Of special importance was the potentiality of all social actors to become elites and legitimately articulate orientations in all spheres of social life—political, cultural, economic and the like. The combination of these ideological premises and structure of elites, together with some crucial organisational aspects of American polities, such as its federalism and the structure of its parties, explain some of the general characteristics of American protest movements in general and of the failure of socialism in them in particular.[18]

The American case exemplifies the different innovative potentials inherent in Western civilisations as carried and articulated by different primary and secondary elite groups. These potentialties were always varied, heterogeneous and often moved in different directions, depending upon concrete historical situations that facilitated or favoured some lines of actualisation as against others. Analysis of these issues in Western societies forms the substance of the following chapters.

Notes

1. See in greater detail S. N. Eisenstadt, 'A Sociological Analysis of Comparative Civilisations, The Development and Direction of a Research Programme', Jerusalem, Harry S. Truman Research Institute, 1986. See S. N. Eisenstadt, 'The Axial Age, The Emergence of Transcendental Visions and the Rise of Clerics', *European Journal of Sociology*, **23**, 1982, pp. 294–314.
2. K. Jaspers, *Vom Urspruch und Ziel der Geschichite*, Zurich, Artemis-Verlag, 1949.
3. F. Heer, *The Intellectual History of Europe*, New York, Anchor Books, Doubleday, 1968; J. K. O'Dea, T. F. O'Dea and C. Adams, *Religion and Man: Judaism, Christianity and Islam*, New York, Harper and Row, 1972; A. von Harnack, *The Mission and Expansion of Christianity in the First Three Countries*, London, Williams and Norgete, 1908; E. Troeltsch, *The Social Teaching of the Christian Churches*, New York, Macmillan, 1931.
4. M. Bloch, *Feudal Society*, London, Routledge and Kegan Paul, 1962.
5. J. Prawer and S. N. Eisenstadt, 'Feudalism', *International Encyclopedia of the Social Sciences*, New York, Macmillan and the Free Press, 1968, Vol. V; pp. 393–403; O. Brunner 'Feudalismus—Ein Beitrag zur Begriffageschichte', in idem, *Neue Wage der Verfassunge-und-Sozialgeschichte*, Gottingen, Vandenhoeck and Ruprecht, 1968; M. M. Cam, 'Medieval Representation in Theory and Practice', in *Speculum*, **29**, 1954; E. Lousse, *La Societe d'Ancien Regime: Organisations et Representations Corporatives*, Louvain, Presses Universitaires, 1943; H. E. Hallam, 'The Medieval Social Picture', pp. 28–50 in E. Kamenka and R. S. Neale, (eds.), *Feudalism, Capitalism and Beyond*, London, Edward Arnold, 1975.
6. Bloch, *Feudal Society*; Brunner, 'Feudalismus'; P. Anderson, *Passages from Antiquity to Feudalism, Lineages of the Absolutist State*, London, New Left Books, 1974.
7. S. N. Eisenstadt, *Social Differentiation and Stratification*, Glenview, Scott-Foreman, 1971.
8. R. Mounier, *Les Hierachies Sociales de 1450 a nos Jours*, Paris, PUF, 1969; Eisenstadt, *Social Differentiation*.
9. J. O. Lindsay, 'The Social Classes and the Foundation of the State', in J. O. Lindsay, (ed.), *New Cambridge Modern History*, Cambridge, Cambridge University Press, 1957.
10. Bloch, *Feudal Society*, pp. 283–305.
11. M. Weber, *The City*, New York, Collier Macmillan, 1957.
12. C. Tilly, ed., *The Formation of National States in Western Europe*, Princeton, Princeton University Press, 1975 (especially the article by S. Rokkan, 'Dimensions of State Formation and Nation Building'); J. LeGoff, (ed.), *Heresies et Sociétés, Civilisations et Sociétés*, Paris, Mouton, 1968; R. Forster and J. Greene, eds., *Preconditions of Revolution in Early Modern Europe*, Baltimore, Johns Hopkins University Press, 1970; A. L. Moote, 'The Preconditions of Revolution in Early Modern Europe, Did They Really

Exist?' *Canadian Journal of History*, **3** 1972; V. Rutenberg, 'Revoltes ou revolutions en Europe aux XIV–XV siecles', *Annales E.S.C.*, **27**, 1973; M. Cohn, *The Pursuit of The Millenium*, New York, Harper, 1961; P. Anderson, *Passages*.

13. M. Weber, *The Protestant Ethic and the Spirit of Capitalism*, New York, Scribner's Sons, 1958; S. N. Eisenstadt, *The Protestant Ethic and Modernization*, New York, Basic Books, 1968.

14. B. Voegelin, *Order and History*, Baton Rouge, Lousiana State University Press; K. Mannheim, *Man and Society*, London: Routledge and Kegan Paul, 1935; J. Habermas, *Towards a Rational Society*, Boston, Beacon Press, 1960; C. Kerr, *Marshall, Marx and Modern Times. The Multi-Dimensional Society*, Cambridge, Cambridge University Press, 1969; I. G. Mesthene, *Technological Change*. Cambridge, Harvard University Press, 1970.

15. These potentialities of *entzauberung* or disenchantment from worldly pursuits are analysed in S. N. Eisenstadt, *Tradition, Change and Modernity*, New York, John Wiley and Sons, 1973.

16. See in greater detail S. N. Eisenstadt and L. Roniger, *Patrons, Clients and Friends*, Cambridge, Cambridge University Press, 1984.

17. A. de Tocqueville, *Democracy in America*, New York, Vintage Press, 1966.

18. It might be worthwhile to have a brief comparative glance at Japan—another great capitalist industrial society—in which it is also impossible to talk about socialism in the European sense despite the existence of a socialist party. Nevertheless, the sources of this similarity are different. Japan presents an opposite situation to the American one. In the latter it was the absence of hierarchical civilisatory premises that explains at least partially the strong relative weakness of socialist movements. In Japan, the relative weakness of such movements is explained by the continuous relative predominance of the vertical hierarchical conceptions and the closely related predominance of strong vertical status orientations, and the concomitant weakness (even within the post World War II democratic state) of egalitarian conceptions within the political realm.

2 The French nation-state: continuities, transformations, and centre formation

Adam Seligman

The purpose of this study is to trace the development of the French nation-state along a particular line of inquiry, from its emergence from the feudal structure to its crystallisation during the period of the Third Republic. Through the study of basic cultural orientations and the modes of their articulation by different elite groups, we will attempt to understand how the interactions between various value orientations, cultural frameworks and institutional structures, contributed to the crystallisation of the social and political centre in post-revolutionary France.

Late feudal developments

Following the disintegration of the Carolingian Empire, a unique French pattern of intricate hierachical feudal structure developed which consisted of multiple layers of subinfeudalisation, and resulted in extreme territorial disunity.[1] From among the multiple and autonomous provincial powers, the Duchy of France and the Capetian monarchy emerged as the principal wielders of political power in the twelfth and thirteenth centuries. Amidst marked economic progress, mainly in extensive land reclamation and the emergence of urban centres, the monarchic centre proceeded along a path of centralisation and territorial consolidation that lasted until the outbreak of the Hundred Years War. In the course of these changes, strong ties and coalitions developed between the monarchy and the urban centres against houses of nobility. Cities grew in importance as social centres, and the merchant strata emerged to become a new, functional and relatively autonomous elite, with a high degree of solidarity and associated with the political monarchic elites.

The conflict between the political and religious centres of the late thirteenth and early fourteenth centuries ended with the triumph of the political monarchic centre, under Philip the Fair, over Pope Boniface VIII, thus firmly limiting the power of the Roman Catholic Church within the broad centre framework.

Finally, the early fourteenth century witnessed the emergence of the Estates-General. First summoned in 1302, by the middle of the century the urban middle strata had reached a firm position of participation within the ruling coalition. The representatives of the Estates-General retained this power until the middle of the fifteenth century, when the Valois rulers emerged out of the anarchy of the Hundred Years War and enabled the monarchic component of the centre to gain enough power to free itself of its dependence on the urban centres.[2]

Transformations in the sixteenth century

Sixteenth century France, like other European countries, was marked by the age of the 'new monarchies'. In France this period was characterised by:

(1) the introduction of Roman law by the Valois rulers;
(2) the beginning of a centralised government;
(3) the consolidation of all the medieval vassal provinces under a single sovereign;
(4) The decline of aristocratic status, prestige and power, and the resultant effect on the aristocracy's position within the central coalition. Part of the general restructuring of the seigneurial role, the seigneurie's decreasing economic inviolability, and the growth of the *noblesse de robe* were related to the growth of urban and bourgeois strata groups;[3]
(5) The development of a coalition of interlocking groups, which slowly crystallised over the years into a strata grouping, and eventually came to control the venues of power—from the civil services to the administration of justice, and from the local courts to the Paris parliament. These groups were characterised by a high degree of internal solidarity; a growing differentiation from broader strata groups and collectivities; limited autonomy from the royal centre; an increasing tendency to bar access to their status position; and strong orientations to power.

All these developments took place within a very particular geopolitical framework. Following Stein Rokkan[4], it is possible to analyse this framework by which state building and territorial consolidation were linked. The success of the latter was determined in part by the French core area which possessed both the necessary geographic distance northward from Rome, and the necessary geopolitical distance westward from the belt of trade cities, to gain sufficient economic political autonomy and power to command resources from the disintegrating peripheral remnants of the Carolingian Empire.

The consolidation of the pre-absolutist centre had two important consequences affecting the periphery and existing sub-centres. First, the process of territorial integration and administrative centralisation marked the beginning of centre permeation of the countryside, which lasted until the nineteenth century. The Paris region constituted the core area and remained so; its exproporiation of the surrounding territory and its attributes as a social and political centre (where the symbols and structure of the social order were forged) became permanent features of French social life. Second, the creation of a standing army and levy of nationwide tax—the 'taille'—furthered the avenues of centre penetration, extraction and control of periphal areas and population. During the first half of the sixteenth century, the two primary elements of centralisation, power and extortive mechanisms were the 'compagnies d'ordonnance'—the kernel of a regular army and the 'taille des gens d'armes'—the first nationwide tax.[5] On the fiscal and military levels these freed the monarchic centre from the prior constraints of the medieval structure. The absolutist centre was to develop on the basis of the power these two institutional developments granted the Valois monarchy.

The social structure of absolutist France: orientations and institutional characteristics

In the realm of state-formation, the two important derivatives of the transformations of the sixteenth century lie in the crystallisation of the absolutist centre and the growth and impingement of the Huguenot collectivity both on the centre and on society as a whole.

In the period between the Fronde (1648–53) and the Revolution of 1789, the absolutist centre crystallised through a number of institutional mechanisms, which were to have a strong impact on social life.[6] Among these mechanisms, both the *paullette* which turned the sale of offices in the State apparatus into heritable property in exchange for an annual payment of a small percentage of their value) and the system of *Intendants* (royal officers answerable only to the Crown) played a major role in reorganising social life during the period of absolutist rule.[7]

The institutionalisation of these measures within the political and

social framework of the French State had many longstanding implications in the realms of centre institutions and centre–periphery relations. These implications were felt also in more general societal orientations. They limited the power of the aristocracy within the centre
coalition and brought about the later form of 'fusion' between the upper
status groups of the *noblesse de robe* and the traditional *noblesse de'epee*.
This subtle form of political and social strata assimilation resulted in the
robe officers attaining leadership among the nobility. It was nevertheless based on a continuing working alliance between the two groups
within the nobility, structured around the defence of aristocractic
privilege.[8] The results of this later development affected the structuring
of collective development, especially in the realm of centre–periphery
relations in a number of ways. First, it aided the process whereby
capitalist forces penetrated the French social structure in the guise of
'feudal remnants'. Second, it provided for the perpetuation of aristocratic values throughout the social structure, as the middle strata did not
develop autonomous social orientations. Third, it hindered the growth
and development of commercial orientations among middle strata
groups.[9] This led to a situation in which the State took an active part in
furthering industrial enterprises and initiating and developing projects
for which private capital was lacking (mostly under Colbert's mercantil-
ist ventures). Thus, another area of State control and regulation was
delineated, and the process of 'industrialisation from above' that
defined one step in the French process of modernisation was initiated.
Fourth, it made for certain limitations in the process of upward
mobility, and hindered the penetration of non-ascriptive criteria for
membership in the national community. Finally, it enabled the process
of state building and collectivity structuring to develop more through
the offices of the absolutist centre (in this case, its administrative
framework), than through the mutual interaction of broader social
groups and elites.[10]

The consequent socio-political centre was defined by a number of
salient institutional characteristics. These were namely, the early and
relatively extensive penetration of the territorial periphery; the interdependence of the centre's political and religious elements; the centre's
ever-increasing autonomy and distinctiveness from the periphery—a
distinctiveness measured symbolically, institutionally and geographi-
cally, with Paris representing their focus; the relatively limited integration of cultural elites into the centre, with the process of state building
and centre construction carried out in large part by the centre and its
administrative elites; the development of strictly regulated, non-
autonomous and limited access of groups to the centres of power and

prestige; the relative segregation and differentiation of elites and orientations; the only minimal development of secondary elites and centres; the political deautonomisation of secondary and protesting elites; and the breaking of intra- and inter-strata links between protesting elites and movements.[11]

Cultural elites, as well as functional groups, developed in close connection with the process of state formation and national consolidation. In their attempts to influence the political and social orders, these religious and intellectual elites played an important role in reorienting some of the basic cultural frameworks and social codes of the French collectivity. Through their articulation of alternative cultural orientations, their relations with both the social centre and social status and strata groups, and the process of their mutual impingement, they were crucial to the crystallisation of the modern social order. Many of the changes in, and particular characteristics of, modes of political legitimacy, protest articulation, centre crystallisation and periphery impingement, as well as the predominant cultural orientations articulated within the French collective, can be traced to the specific dynamics of elite impingement in the pre-Revolutionary French society.

Thus, while the centre elites propounded the orientational perspectives outlined above, other groups of protesting elites emerged, which articulated a different set of cultural orientations, symbolic premises and models of social action. The process of impingement on and mode of incorporation by the centre of three such groups—the Humanists, Huguenots and Jansenists—provide examples of the dynamics of social action in the French absolutist social structure.

The Humanist elites provided the beginnings of those secular orientations which often develop as a society emerges from the traditional structures: a strong interweaving of orientation to salvation; emphasis on autonomous access to the attributes of salvation; definition of attributes of the mediating agencies between centre and periphery dissociated from ascriptive criteria; development of emphasis on the attributes of individual conscience and laicisation of learning. In line with the previously noted characteristics of the centre, a specific mode of incorporating Humanist orientations developed. This incorporation tended to de-emphasise these orientations and re-integrate Humanist elites into the structures of the Church, in a manner that furthered both the segregation of elites and the dominance of the centre itself.[12]

While advancing the perspectives articulated by the Humanists, members of the Huguenot collective related them to the socio-political realm, thereby stressing an active and committed attitude towards, and participation in, the social and cultural order, change, a conception of legitimate access to the major attributes of the social and cosmic orders, and the development of a strong individualist emphasis, especially in the realm of morality.[13] As with the Humanists, the centre incorporated these orientations only to a limited degree, thus leading to the continual segregation of elites, the perpetuation of hierarchic principles of social ordering, the conception of a 'natural' economy, the continuing dependence of the nobility on the crown and, crucially, the continuity of orientations stressing the 'givenness' of the social order and non-participatory orientations.[14]

Finally, the growth and development of the Jansenist movement throughout the latter half of the seventeenth century, provided the focal point for the coalescence of various intellectual, political and status elites that were excluded from the centre's frame of reference.[15] Moreover, it was these elites that carried some of the basic orientations around which those social forces we often equate with the process of modern change tended to coalesce. This was particularly true of their development of a'new morality', whose effect on the values and mores of the bourgeois class as a whole were studied in the works of Bernard Groethuysen and Franz Borkenau.[16] The continued failure of the centre to incorporate the Jansenist elite (or their cultural orientations) led to the growth of a politicised Jansenism of protest, a process which reached its culmination in the Grand Remonstrance of 1753.

In the most general terms, a number of important characteristics can be said to have developed in the sphere of elite interaction in pre-revolutionary France:

(1) A tendency existed among certain groups of secondary elites towards the coalescence of protest demands;

(2) The high degree of distinction between the centre and periphery, and the limited nature of access to the centre, led these cultural and religious elites to orient their activities towards the political spheres;

(3) These elites evinced a strong tendency to impinge on the political sphere and to claim an autonomous role in articulating its basic premises;

(4) Both Huguenots and Jansenists tended to develop a high degree of association with broader strata groups and thereby became important articulators of models of collective identity;

(5) On the whole, the centre succeeded, on the organisational level, in breaking the intra- and inter-strata links between protest movements and elites, in condensing their symbolic autonomy and restricting the cultural orientations carried by the different elite structures.

Elites who carried protest orientations did, however, influence modes of collective action, and in so doing, led to an even greater distinction between centre and periphery. One aspect of this was evident in the transformation of protest themes in the sixteenth century, and the construction and articulation by the Huguenots of an ideology of protest and resistance.[17] This crucial element in the legitimation of protest and resistance (whether of inferior magistrates or the body of the people) was articulated as part of an alternative conception of the socio-cultural order, and marked a major step towards the articulation of a political ideology of resistance to ruling powers. First articulated by the Huguenot religio-political elites, this transformation in attitudes towards resistance and modes of protest was an important result of the dynamics of Huguenot impingement and centre response in the sixteenth century. Moreover, together with the new ideology of protest, a new set of cultural orientations towards direct and autonomous access to the social and cosmic centres and a more egalitarian structuring of the social hierarchy were articulated. The elites 'carrying' these orientations were characterised by a strong interweaving of orientations and by virtue of this important characteristic, were dissociated from the elites of the centre.

The mode of protest incorporation was no less crucial than protest itself for the later development of collective life. For whereas the centre ultimately incorporated some strata elites, such as the Huguenots, the conceptions and orientations they carried were not fully integrated into the centre's social conception. The limited incorporation of the wider cultural orientations of protest, together with the centre's failure to legitimise the existence of autonomous symbolic orders and social sub-centres, resulted in the continuing divergence between cultural, and political-administrative frameworks. For while the political framework remained tied to cultural codes and orientations defined, on the whole, by tradition-bound criteria, the cultural frameworks— whether Jesuit or Jansenist pedagogical institutions, seventeenth century salon society or the coteries formed in the coffee houses in the Rive Gauche—all tended to further the social permeation and acceptance of non-traditional codes and orientations.

Finally, the social structuralisation of the cultural elite groups beyond the parameters of the centre, influenced the very nature of protest articulation and incorporation within *ancien regime* society. Elite integration, when instituted, tended to be based on personal patronage. As a result, the influence of elite incorporation on the basic symbols and structures of the centre remained limited. Thus, as egalitarian and individualistic orientations began to permeate the social structure, challenging hierarchic centre principles, no directional perspectives capable of orientating themselves to periphery demands developed within the centre frameworks.

The development of a revolutionary situation

The dynamics of elite impingement and collectivity formation, which developed with the consolidation of the territorial unit under the absolutist regime, occurred within an institutional framework undergoing a process of change and dislocation. Changes in the economic sphere, and the rise of new strata groups and new entrepreneurial elites which sought access to centre orders and positions of power and prestige, were among the important developments of eighteenth century France. The inability of the centre to integrate these social groups into its symbolic and institutional orders was, as has often been noted, a primary element in the development of the revolutionary situation.

The failure of Turgot's reform measures (focused on tax return, free grain trade and the suppression of corporate bodies) was indicative of this inability to reorient centre structures.[18] This failure was due essentially to the opposition of privileged groups, members of the centre coalition, to broadening the allocative mechanisms of society. This opposition, in fact, reveals one of the major structural weaknesses of the eighteenth century centre. As we have seen above, the traditional centre consisted of status groups of functional/economic elites whose interests lay primarily in the perpetuation of non-capitalist economic orientations (such as seigneurial rights and propriety offices, and the perpetuation of a tax system whose revenues came from the lower orders). The rigidity of the traditional centre tended to set major sections of different strata and status groups and important segments of the dominant class itself against the centre, and ultimately against the total structure of ancient regime society.

These developments were related to the emergence of a new stratum in eighteenth century France. 'No longer feudal in the political or judicial sense . . . it was not capitalist either—not in the entrepreneurial and not in the Marxist sense'.[19] This stratum was basically an unified dominant class. But one of the its most distinctive features was its lack of autonomy and heavy dependence on the monarchic political centre. Its dependence on the State had grown with the displacement of the medieval stratification system of orders and estates through the centralisation pressures of the monarchy.[20]

This dependence led to a process of state building and centre construction defined largely in terms of the growing centrality of the royal centre (as opposed to England, for instance, where it was defined in terms of the fusion of the centre with the ruling class, or dominant strata group), and resulted in what was perhaps its prime contradiction and structural weakness. For in the prevailing conditions, the only bodies capable of representative functions, of articulating periphery protest or demands for reform—in short, the only barriers against excessive royal authority—were the old corporate bodies: aristocratic, professional, judicial, urban or provincial. Yet it was precisely the institutional autonomy of these bodies and their role as articulators of alternative (mostly traditional) models and modes of social action that had to be broken in order to further the process of periphery integration in the construction of the nation–state. It was, moreover, precisely these bodies that offered the greatest resistance to any far-reaching changes in the distribution of wealth, power of prestige, and they were consequently the primary obstacles to any progressive, gradual change in the later course of the eighteenth century.

The inability of the centre to regulate and mediate between the developing and emerging social groups, to integrate them into a common institutional framework, or to legitimise new and developing foci of collective national identity, resulted in an essentially fragile social centre. Its structural weakness lay in its inability to develop and maintain an institutional structure capable of absorbing those forces of modern change that lay beyond its own initial premises, either on the symbolic or the institutional level. The institutional and administrative isolation of the centre, under the ministries of Mazarin, Richelieu and Colbert, while crucial to the development of a state structure, ultimately were disastrous, in that they isolated this structure from a number of modernising social groups engendered by the process of nation–formation.

The social contradictions within the absolutist regime were moreover related to contradictions within the economic structure. These can be summed up as the continuing restrictive relations between commerce and the nascent industries, and the socio-political structure of agrarian-traditional France, which was imperio-feudal in nature. French agriculture remained 'backward' in comparison to both English agriculture and French commerce and industry. Regional specialisation was slow to develop and the introduction of new agricultural techniques, developed between the sixteenth and eighteenth centuries in England and Holland, made only limited progress. This was due to three factors: first, the structure of landholdings—approximately one-third of the land was held by small-holding peasantry who were unable to finance improvements, the rest was owned by a landed upper class whose remaining seigneurial rights stood in the way of any progress towards the consolidation and national organisation of substantial holdings; second, the heavy burden of taxation, which fell mainly on the peasantry; and third, the increase in gross agricultural production during mid-eighteenth century, due to good harvests, which brought high prices and higher rents to the large landholders, thereby obscuring the need for crucial structural changes.

These structural characteristics of French agriculture restricted industrial growth and resulted in a recurring cycle of agricultural crises and famine. In the years from 1600 to 1630, 1660 to 1690, and 1730 to 1770, economic expansion ended in slackened demand and spiralling bread prices. It was precisely this type of economic crisis, together with the political crises of 1788–1789, that proved to be the beginning of transformative revolutionary process.[21] In more general and comparative terms, it may be said that while the centre succeeded in establishing the structural prerequisites for nation–state formation (through its break with the feudal social order), it remained tied to traditional orientations and codes that were incongruent with the emerging social forces, strata groups and orientations. The premises of the traditional order upon which the centre rested were inadequate to encompass the major social and historical changes that accompanied the process of early modern development.[22]

As a result the emergence of a national–collective conception within the different elite groups and its permeation to broader strata groups developed in an asymptotic relation to that of the political and cultural centre. This type of historical trajectory was caused primarily by the transformation marking the absolutist phase of centre consolidation which was characterised by increased limitation in the channels of access to the centre. As the cultural orientations of society began to change, under the impact of different elite groups and protest movements, the premises of centre existence increasingly lost their viability within the social framework. As the codes of autonomous access to the social and cosmic centres gained in saliency, they tended to undermine and dislocate the premises of the existing social structure. The closed nature of the centre, its strong predilection to power and increasing limitation on the plurality of prestige, precluded the incorporation of the different protest orientations within centre symbols. The failure of the centre to incorporate the basic dimensions of protest within the core components of the socio-political order was the ultimate cause of its collapse and of the emergence of the revolutionary situation.

Revolutionary transformations

Just as the symbolic dissociation between the centre and periphery was one of the prime structural elements leading to the development of a revolutionary situation, so the history of the French polity from 1789 was one of growing attempts to obliterate those differences. In fact, what distinguishes the French Revolution from earlier moments of protest, such as the Fronde or the Holy League, was precisely the fact that it made a conscious attempt to reshape the social order through a strong emphasis on the building of instutitions and the structuring of the collectivity.

This thrust towards centre and institution building occurred against the background of a high degree of rupturing, of both wide-ranging structural dislocation and ideological discontinuity with pre-revolutionary society. These changes, together with changes in the principles and symbols of legitimation, in the rules governing access to different markets and use of resources, and in the bases of social hierarchies, all contributed to what was to be the defining problem of nineteenth century French society: i.e., the construction of both symbols and institutions capable of establishing consensual norms of social interaction and models of social order.[23]

The nature of the centre which emerged after the Revolution was of fundamental importance in defining the post-revolutionary social order. Both in its symbolic and institutional orders, the post-revolutionary centre constituted not only the major moment in the consolidation of the French nation-state, but also a paradigmatic referent for defining ensuing breakthroughs to a modern social order.[24] The major characteristics of this modern social order rested on the radical transformation of the role of protest in socio-political restructuring. For with the Revolution, both the symbols and the concrete demands of protest became basic components of the centre's social and political symbolism. Protest was thus institutionalised as a prime component of centre construction and, more importantly in the legitimation of protesting elites, as articulators of collective models and goals.

The effects of this development were felt in the radical restructuring of the society's central institutional and symbolic spheres. The basic symbols of the centre crystallised around a new set of assumptions on the nature of participation and membership, in the collective principles of political legitimation, models of collective identity and the broader purpose and meaning of collective goals. These were apparent in the search for new principles of social ordering and justice articulated in terms of non-traditional set of values, in finding new symbols of a common identity which would combine the universalistic and Utopian moments of the Revolution with solutions to the specific problems of nineteenth century French modernisation, and in re-establishing non-attenuated relations between individuals, and between them and the central institutional frameworks.[25]

The new assumptions and symbols of the centre emerged concomitant with important changes in its institutional orders. Most important among these was the possibility of reshaping the relations between the centre and the periphery through the activity of periphery groups and their impingement on the social centre. In opening up channels of access to the centre, through the concept of 'citoyen' and the principle of the franchise the Revolution opened up the possibility of a continuing process of periphery impingement and centre permeation. Moreover, it was this radical restructuring of the venues of access to the centre that lent it one of its basic characteristics: the continuing attempt of different groups on the periphery to broaden the scope of participation in and the channels of access to, the centre, and to change and reformulate their social and cultural content.

In the sphere of cultural orientations, the effects of the Revolution were felt primarily in the following changes, which, when institutionalised, provided the basic pattern of elite impingement on the centre, as well as of centre–periphery relations throughout the process of nineteenth century national consolidation:

(i)   the articulation of a new basis of political legitimation, no longer based on sacred or primordial criteria, but redefined in terms of popular representation and accountability to the broader collective;

(ii) the establishment of new venues of access to the centre, based on the concept of citizenship and the principles of the franchise;

(iii) the articulation of new modes of collective identity encompassed in the concept of equality before the law;

(iv) the growing definition of collective solidarity in terms of membership within the territorial collective rather than in ascriptive or religious communities.

The combined result of this revolutionary reorientation was that membership in the collectivity became a title to access to the centre. On both the symbolic and institutional planes this represented a crucial rupture with traditional conception of society and centre–periphery relations. This radical break with tradition, furthermore, coincided with the emerging conception of a collective national identity which was distinct from the ruling centre.

An increased social differentiation and changes in stratification structure of society in the wake of the Revolution resulted in the development of new functional and professional elites not embedded in fixed ascriptive frameworks. As a result, the above noted orientations were articulated by new structures of functional, political and cultural elites who had greater access to the centre, and participated in the reconstruction of the centre and the social order. Among these, new groups of industrial elites, as well as financiers, civil servants, wealthier lawyers and journalists, were prominent.[26] The increasing permeation and secularisation of the State educational apparatus throughout the century led to the growth and development of an educated intelligentsia such as had not existed in the years of the *ancien regime*. These intellectuals came to play an increasingly important role as carriers of different orientations and as articulators of collective identity and models of solidarity, thus, to a large extent, taking over the position formerly held by the local clergy.[27]

Finally, new structures of political elites, initially thrown up by the revolutionary process, emerged. These elites, which had been marginal to the dominant structures and ruling coalitions of the *ancien regime*, came to structure one of the most salient characteristics of post-revolutionary society: the connection between political activity—articulated in highly-principled ideological terms—and broad strata groups. They served as links between rapidly mobilising groups on the periphery and the centre, bringing them into the participatory process, and connecting their concrete demands with the broader process of institution-building and centre formation.

The revolution engendered additional radical changes in a number of primary institutional spheres. The administrative reorganisation of the political centre for example, saw the emergence of a modern legislative system in the National Constituent Assembly of 1789–91, the Legislative Assembly of 1791–2 and the Convention of 1792–4. These, together with the institutional apparatus of the new state edifice which crystallised during the first Empire, permitted the continuing integration of political elites within the State structure. This method of elite incorporation ensured the continued existence of the organs of the State structure throughout the nineteenth century, irrespective of the instability of any particular political regime.[28] Concomitant with these developments was the centre's propensity to intensify its permeation of the periphery and extractive capacities, and the centrality of Paris to the economic, social and political life of the territorial collective. This process of centre aggrandizement was furthered by a marked increase in government bureaucracy and the nationalisation of the administrative mechanisms of the State apparatus. As a result, a highly differentiated institutional structure which was based on a centralisation of policy with specific political goals developed. This structure extended the scope of central, legal, administrative and political activities and furthered their penetration into all realms of society.[29]

The periphery, too, was subject to a number of changes. These were evident in various spheres, primarily the economic, where changes in the nature of land holdings led to growth of a strong landed middle class. The first half of the century witnessed the growth and consolidation of different economic groups into a powerful middle class. Mid-century industrialisation led to the growth of an industrial working class, together with critical demographic shifts, urbanisation, and economic, cultural and political–territorial unification. Centre penetration and extraction of periphery resources also brought about the increased political mobilisation of the periphery, the development of strata-consciousness, and a greater propensity to impinge on the centre with political, social and economic demands.[30]

The dynamics of post-revolutionary reconstruction and the problems of crystallisation of the centre

In terms of both its symbolic and institutional orders, the nineteenth century French centre was structured by the models of centre symbols and institutions which emerged during the Revolution and the period of the Consulate and the First Empire.[31] The emergence of new institutional structures capable of regulating the major dimensions of social existence, was, however, tied to pervasive problems in maintaining a symbolic centre able to evoke legitimacy, give meaning and articulate the fundamental principles of social order.

The variety of political regimes succeeding one another over the nineteenth century reflected the attenuated nature of the commitment the centre evoked from either broad strata groups or society's elites. The legacy of *ancien regime* orientations, existing side by side with the 'revolutionary' orientations of 1789, continually militated against the crystallisation of strong centre orientated along secular lines, with an accepted framework for mutual centre–periphery impingement and interaction.[32] Similarly, the developing contradictions between the symbolic premises of the Revolution and the institutional structures of post-revolutionary society also constituted an obstacle to centre crystallisation. For the Revolution not only overthrew many of the limitations, restrictions, inequalities and injustices of the *ancien regime*, but also sharpened many of the distinctions between centre and periphery. In so doing, it intensified struggles and conflicts at the very intersection (of permeation and impingement) between centre and periphery.[33]

The nexus of the new structuring of centre–periphery relations lay in the changed role of protest following the Revolution. Following its institutionalisation and the incorporation of its symbols as primary centre attributes, protest was oriented towards the construction of new symbolic and institutional boundaries of collective life. The orientations and activities of protesting groups and elites thus became a major mode through which collective action, orientated towards the construction of new symbolic and effective commitments, was undertaken. Through the impingement of protest on the social centre, the framework of subjective orientations was transformed as people became available for new patterns of socialisation and behaviour. This process was exemplified in the crystallisation of new presuppositions on the nature of the social order and its centre; among the most important of which (in the political sphere) were new assumptions on the distribution of resources among social groups and their incorporation into centre orders.[34]

On a concrete level, these themes were articulated as struggles over the nature of various ruling coalitions (constitutional or absolute monarchy, parliamentary democracy or Empire), over the role of the Church in collective life (specifically over its role as an interpreter of collective goals), over the implementation of basic rights (to political organisation, strike and freedom of the press), and over opening the venues of access of broad social groups to major markets of power, prestige and wealth (as exemplified in struggles over taxation policies and in geopolitical periphery protest to the growing centrality of Paris, to the process of linguistic unification).[35]

Carriers of protest

During and after the period of the Restoration, the process of political organisation grew more intense as political elites came to articulate the social demands of different social and occupational groups in political terms.[36] Political elites began to organise in secret societies and clubs and to develop the rudiments of party frameworks.[37] The restructuring of the major dimensions of social life, economic development and

differentiation, urbanisation and social mobility, the structural dislocation of existing groups and the emergence of new occupational groups
and their attempts at impingement on the centre—all led to the
development of broadly-based and orientated political organisations.
This development saw a fuller articulation of both class orientations and
political ideology among the political elite groups.[38]

During this period, it was primarily the different structures of elites,
political, intellectual and religious, which articulated collective models
of solidarity, the modes of legitimacy and the principles of the symbolic
ordering of social life. The orientations carried out by these elites varied
from extremely traditional to revolutionary. The opposition of the
clergy to secular intellectuals, of ultra-montane political elites to their
republican counterparts, of conservative to radical republicans—all
carrying different conceptions of the nature of the centre, its attributes
and modes of access—thus became the crux of the social and political
struggles in nineteenth century France.

Traditional elites

The more tradition-oriented elites maintained varying degrees of commitment to the social codes and orientations of the *ancien regime*, a
commitment which itself changed with the progress of modernisation.[39]
The move from the Ultras to the Legitimists, and the growth of the
Orleanist party at the expense of the Legitimists, are examples of this
process. The more responsive these elites were to the growing permeation of republican and democratic orientations within the collective, the
greater was their political saliency. Bonapartism, though not traditional
in the sense of being monarchist, represents the most progressive of
these elite structures—open in its orientations and attempting to
represent all the strata groups in the collective.

These elites varied *vis-à-vis* their relationship with the centre. Consequently, each elite (Legitimist, Ultra, Orleanist and Bonapartist) at one
time represented the focal point of the political centre. Once it had lost
its predominant place in the centre coalition, none ever regained the
degree of political power or ascendancy it had had. The Revolutions of
1830 and 1848, the defeat at Sedan and the Commune of 1871, all
represented the repudiation of a particular centre conception. The
failures of the different regimes were steps towards the consolidation of
a democractic nation–state. With the progressive widening of access to
the centre and broadening of participation established by each revolution, the modes of collective solidarity articulated by the previous

centre became less and less tenable. Out of power, these elites continued to impinge on the social structure and in so doing established the basis for the growth of the modern right in France. The continuation from the Dreyfus Affair and the *Action Française* through the Vichy regime of a traditional right-wing political orientation (re-articulated in the 1890's as a type of nationalism—once the province of the left), points to the important role these elites played in modelling collective orientations.[40]

Revolutionary and socialist elites

The different structures of revolutionary political elites varied in their degree of identification with and commitment to both the ideals and goals of the Revolution itself, and the institutional framework which crystallised throughout the nineteenth century and sought to implement these ideals in social life.[41]

One of the major areas in which these different orientations were apparent was that of the respective elite structures' political orientations. These were best represented by the differences between Jaures' parliamentary socialism, Blanqui's attempted coups and the syndicalist general strike. Each signifies, in essence, a different degree of commitment to the centre, as well as a different conception of political action. Moreover, the different degrees of commitment to the centre were manifest in the varying levels of participation. In their commitment to the centre and conception of democratic, representative political action, the socialists brought thousands of citizens into the political process. The socialists' successful political mobilisation of the mass urban workers, large sections of the peasantry and rural workers was not matched by developments among the anarcho–syndicalists. Although the latter instilled a heightened political awareness among its membership and supporters, this did not lead to participation in the practice of the democratic system. However, identification with the Revolution and acceptance of the parameters it provided for national identity, marked, to a great extent, the limits of identification with and commitment to the Republican centre.

Thus, given the importance of the revolutionary tradition in France, the breadth of the socialist movement and its elites and the affirmative echo their orientations found among different groups within society (specifically among members of the middle class and the intellectuals), the centre of the Third Republic could not have been constituted without a minimum of legitimation granted and commitment elicited from socialist elites. However, although some socialist orientations and elites were incorporated into the centre structure, the basic model of class symbolism, of course remained, peripheral to the centre's social conception. In the light of this, and in contrast to elites within the socialist political movement proper, many of the different revolutionary and working class elites maintained only a limited degree of commitment to the centre and were not incorporated within its institutional structure. These were the elites of the syndicalist movement and the conspiratorial groups whose orientations were grounded in class symbolism and the irreconcilable conflict between social classes.[42]

Republican elites

Finally, the stability and crystallisation of the post-revolutionary centre rested in no small measure on the successful incorporation of those orientations which were first articulated during the 1789 Revolution into the collective as a whole, and especially into the structures of its elites.[43] This process was the result of the impingement of various republican elites on the existing centre orders (especially during the Second Empire), broader strata groupings and other elite structures. Especially important in this process was the role played by such groups as teachers (the *institutiers*), intellectuals (writers such as Victor Hugo, poets such as Lamartine and professors such as Quinet and Michelet), journalists, and the different groups of social reformers and Utopians[44]—all of whom carried republican 'revolutionary' orientations to different status groups and elites.

The close connection between the demands and ideological premises of the late nineteenth century republicans and those of the 1789 Revolution were thus a crucial characteristic of republican protest, politics and indeed, 'belief'. The revolutionary orientations of 1789 were re-articulated by the republicans of the late nineteenth century in order to meet current demands and needs. One such issue of particular relevance at the time was that of ministerial responsibility. On this issue, as on many others, republicans elicited legitimacy and mobilized support by re-stating the social doctrines of 1789.

In drawing legitimacy from past revolutionary tradition, and in positing the 1789 Revolution as the symbolic centre (yet to be institutionally realised), republican protest presented a viable alternative vision of society, its centre and social order, to that existing under the different political regimes of the nineteenth century. This alternative received a growing degree of acceptance among different social groups and was closely bound to the new sense of collective identity. In contrast to the traditional elites that wished to return to the pre-revolutionary social order, or to the socialist and revolutionary elites that were only partially committed to the political principles of the 'Declaration of the Rights of Man', the republicans articulated a political doctrine whose symbolic elements were already accepted by most (though not all) of the population. By uniting the political and social principles of the Revolution with the new parameters of national identity it had engendered, the republicans gained strength and support. Most importantly (especially in the context of the Franco–Prussian War), they reaffirmed the national identity articulated during the Revolution, and tied that identity to the political principles which, in effect, underlay the notion of popular sovereignty. Republican protest was thus a constitutive element in centre formation. In the process of their impingement with other groups of elites—monarchists, clergy and the elites of the left—the republicans came, through the presentation of specific demands, to articulate a new model of collective goals.

Incorporation of elites, protest and the crystallisation of the centre

The crystallisation of the post-revolutionary centre rested to a large extent on the emergence of elite groups capable of representing the needs of wide-ranging and diverse social groups and strata in their symbols and institutional programmes. Moreover, the degree of incorporation in the post-revolutionary centre of the above-mentioned elites, as well as of their orientations, was structured by these needs. The rejection of traditionalist elites, in both the revolutions of 1830 and 1848, and of their attempts, in different ways, to mediate the symbolic and institutional changes wrought by the Revolution, was directly related to their narrow conception of the parameters of the collective and their deep embedment in increasingly isolated strata and status groupings. Indeed, the very success of Orleanism (as opposed to Ultracist or Legitimist political elites), lay in its relative 'openness'—both to parliamentary democracy, as well as to achieved, rather than ascribed, criteria as evaluating status positions (thus their strong links with the bourgeoisie). By including a strong parliamentary orientation in their political creed and incorporating different social elites of wealth, birth and intellect, the Orleanists were able to keep monarchism alive within French society.[45]

Similarly, the success of Bonapartism lay in its ability to integrate the demands of different occupational and strata groups, and to present itself as 'above' their conflicting demands.[46] In building their administrative machinery, the Bonapartists drew heavily on the previous Orleanist bureaucracy, integrating it into the new political centre. While this served to strengthen the mechanisms of the State and the process of centre crystallisation, Bonapartism also furthered the construction of a truly national collective. This was evinced in the relative politicisation of the peasantry and the use of the plebiscite. The latter, although it was more formal than real, nevertheless furthered the process of mass participation in collective life.

A similar dynamic of openness versus closure to the needs of the collective as a whole characterised the role played by socialist and other revolutionary elites in the crystallisation of the post-revolutionary centre. For the socialists, the problem was represented by the dual nature of the revolutionary heritage: on the one hand, a particular national collective defining orientation, and on the other, a universalistic orientation with socialist implications. The symbolic and institutional means (such as universal suffrage and a more equitable taxation structure) that were required to establish the new basis of solidarity were instituted in, and became the basis of, the democratic nation-state. Those elements of the revolutionary heritage which served as the basis for the growth of socialist orientations and of the socialist movement were, needless to say, not incorporated to the same extent. In general, the measure of socialist elite incorporation by the centre was a function of the centre's ability to accept socialist orientations (at any given time), and of the willingness of particular revolutionary elite groups to compromise with the Janus-faced nature of their heritage.[47]

Finally, and no less important than the above, was the ability of the republicans to compromise, and to accept the rules of the political game and social pluralism.[48] Lacking the doctrinaire social ideology of either the ultra-right or the socialists, the republicans managed to subsume most ideological differences and conflicts of interest into the broad scheme of acceptance or rejection of the Revolution and its symbolic premises. In so doing, they engendered the minimal consensus needed for centre crystallisation and nation formation. Within the symbolic parameters established by the Revolution, the republicans constructed an institutional order with enough space for manoeuvring between parties, interests and ideologies.[49]

The symbolic elements of the republican synthesis

Throughout the nineteenth century, the French centre was organisationally functional, though weak and ideologically uncrystallised. Its crystallisation rested to a great extent on the construction of a new sense of national identity based on the symbolic premises of the 1789 Revolution. As noted, these constituted one of the major themes of republican rhetoric and demands.

Through their structures of popular political organisation and participation, the republicans attracted different social groups whose broad value orientations had been decisively moulded by the continuing revolutionary traditions. Thus the republicans effectively engendered new *loci* for the coalescence of protest. Peasant demands were joined with the protest of urban workers, and both were linked to the demands of unemployed students and professionals who possessed skills but lacked status and material wealth.[50] Demands for the more equal distribution of national resources were combined with demands for direct access to the centre and increased political participation. Concomitantly, a rising secularism made itself felt in republican orientations. Through the coalescence of these different demands, alternate models of collective norms, social values and centre orientations came to be articulated. In drawing legitimation from the Revolution—legitimation for what in mid-nineteenth century France were far-reaching changes in the social order—the republicans prepared the way for the final consolidation of a new sense of collective solidarity based on the principles and social ideals articulated during the Revolution. This was the '*bloc*' Clemenceau referred to at the end of the nineteenth century. It represented not only the programmes of social reforms (in the conditions of the working man, political access, education, and so on). demanded by the republicans, but also the constitution of a new set of national parameters. The importance of the republican movement, and indeed, its eventual success rested on the sense of identity they articulated between the socio-political principles of the 1789 Revolution and their own organisational structures.[51]

The changing role of the Church

One of the important areas where the effects of this 'synthesis' was felt was in the changing role of the Church in society—a change which reflected the process of national integration and the constitution of new principles and symbols of national identity, membership and solidarity. Of all the conflicts which divided nineteenth century France, perhaps the most divisive was the religious, dividing France into '*la France athee*' and '*la France chretienne*', and crystallising around the following issues:[52]

(1) the secular nature of the State (in concrete struggles over the educational system, or in more symbolic conflicts such as those over the erection of the statue of Voltaire or the benediction of ambulances in 1871);

(2) the social and political actions of the clergy (i.e. their anti-republicanism, which often was stated explicitly);

(3) the growth of ultra-montanism in the Church (especially in the support afforded Pope Pious IX).

Here, too, the ability of the republican elite to compromise and construct institutionalised channels for protest (of various kinds) tended to diffuse even these 'loaded' issues, and to put them on the political agenda as an issue for compromise and bargaining, rather than for revolt and revolution. Cremieux's compromise of 1871 regarding army service for seminarists, as well as the later failure of the *Raillement*, both illustrate the crucial changes in the nature of Church–State relations established through the developing modes of elite interaction.

Thus, though the Church continued to play an important role in structuring collective life—a role which was indeed linked to the continuing instability of the French centre—the Third Republic witnessed a general replacement of ecclesiastical elites by civil ones as the primary carriers of collective models and articulators of collective goals and orientations. The decreasing saliency of the Church was felt in its increasing loss of control over resources and markets (the primary example being education, but also in the loss of its central place in local, specifically rural, politics), as well as in its removal from the symbolic sphere as the principal articulator of collective life. The separation of Church and State was thus a measure of the autonomy gained by political and other elites from dependency on ecclesiastical legitimacy. The successful crystallisation of the republican centre resulted in a general separation between political and ecclesiastical orientations and institutions. Although it was, of course, an important feature in France, this autonomy of the State from ecclesiastical influence was not as complete as, for example, in England. Indeed the Church in France continued to play an important role in political life.

This period witnessed not only a separation of structures, elites and institutions, but also a broad replacement of clerical orders by republican ones. Republican elites and symbols came to replace those of the Church in the area of education, in the structuring of national symbols, in modes of legitimacy and in general orientations.[53] These developments led to the aforementioned change in attitudes and actions of ecclesiastic elites, and their acceptance of existing political symbols, frameworks and channels of access to the centre. This acceptance, together with a minimal degree of commitment to the centre, was not unproblematic, even after the establishment of the Third Republic. For example, the heated debate in parliament and in the streets over the allocation of funds to build the Sacre Coeur, presented by clerical elites as an 'atonement' for the 'sins' of the commune, illustrates two sides of this dynamic: on the one hand, the continuing anti-republicanism of the Church (also manifested in its position against amnesty to the communants) and on the other, its continuing acceptance of institutional channels of protest and presentation of demands. The latter development was however, of central importance in providing for the separation of Church and State and a relatively crystallised and stable centre.

Structural components of national consolidation

The crystallisation of the centre and the emergence of a wide reaching sense of national identity within the territorial unit of nineteenth century France was a product of variegated symbolic and structural factors. Most crucial perhaps, were the major characteristics of stratification restructuring which were felt in the crystallisation of the centre during the Third Republic. These characteristics were: the loss of aristocratic wealth, prestige and power; the acculturation of the peasantry into the national collective; the increased (albeit mediated) legitimation granted to the working class (in terms of participation and membership); and most importantly, the emergence of the 'nouvelle couche sociale'—created by the economic growth of the Second Empire, the development of new techniques and the more complex division of labour in society—together with the emergence of a new professional elite (the capacites).[54] Together, these developments led to the emergence of new dominant strata and status groups which, in contrast to the ruling groups until the Third Republic, maintained an openness of access to, and participation in, the making and remaking of the basic symbols and institutions of the centre. Similarly, despite the conflicting orientations on the nature of the proper social order, a number of structural characteristics of the different elite groups contributed to the eventual crystallisation on an accepted framework of interaction between them. Among these were the different 'metaphysical universe' (to use Richard Wright's phrase)[55] inhabited by such groups as the republicans and Catholics which permitted only a minimum of interaction, and therefore of confrontation and conflict, between them. Concomitantly, multiple networks of cross-cutting ties of religion, friendship, family and profession existed between different elites. These tended not only to mediate the intensity of conflicting socio-cultural orientations, but also furthered a shared conception of social and economic values.

These factors, together with the heterogeneity of coalition members at the elite level (who brought with them different levels of commitment to their joint venture), and the diffusion of power and prestige (and their regulation) among different levels of society, engendered a commitment among different groups and elites both to society at large and to its centre. Furthermore, the particular geopolitical divisions which characterised French nation-building (the centrality of Paris), as well as such factors as the Franco–Prussian War, played an important role in integrating the diverse and often opposing demands of social groups. Thus, the cross-cutting nature of conflict issues—often combining in various forms such diverse issues as family, clan, kinship, religion and politics with geopolitical periphery protest against Parisian centralisation, or inter-regional and class-based conflict—tended, on the local level, to unite elites sharing diverse orientations towards the national collective, and to de-emphasise the importance of overriding 'ideological' issues.

The continual problems political elites encountered in mobilising the mass of the populace for political activity were yet another issue which tended to de-emphasise conflicting ideological premises. Conflicting world-views tended to remain more the province of urban elites than of the rural masses; for the latter, politics were primarily a mode of acculturation, rather than of 'world-building'. Social groups on the elite and mass level were indeed united by a sense of patriotism, rooted in the Revolution (despite their different interpretations of it), as well as in the anti-German sentiment that prevailed during the Franco–Prussian War. Nationalism, with its strong mobilising myths, provided a salient integrating force beyond the ongoing conflicts within society. Nationalism was also felt in the 'negotiability' of many ideological conflicts which were worked out on the elite level. Although their conceptions of the ideal social order varied, the different elites were nevertheless united in their concern for the efficacy of some order, especially during the turbulence of the war of 1871.

Summary: the role of the past

The particularities of the crystallisation of the French centre like much else in republican France, were related to its earlier history and, in part, rooted in prior conflicts and conceits. Certain patterns of protest and beliefs can, in fact, be traced back to early modern French history. For example, certain geographic areas, like the Massif Central, have always been strongholds of religious protest—of Cathars, Albigensians and Protestants.[56] In such areas, the political conflicts of the nineteenth century were defined, more often than not, along religious, rather than political lines. In other areas, a coalescence of traditional Catholic orientations with local and linguistic protest tended to afford particular meaning to political conflicts on a national scale. Some insight into the concrete mechanisms of this dynamic of continuity between historical and modern France may be ascertained by reviewing the overall characteristics of protest over the course of historical development.

There were a number of salient developments in the earlier (pre-revolutionary) period of nation formation which affected the evolution of protest within France. One was the limited incorporation by the centre of the orientations articulated by the Huguenot (and later, Jansenist) religio–political elites. The limited incorporation of these elites and the orientations they carried resulted in a socio-cultural order characterised by weak symbolic and affective commitments to the centre, a limited consensus on common socio-political goals, and an only partial degree of congruence between the cultural and political identities of the territorial populace. This, in turn, increased the potential for protest to orient itself beyond the parameters of the existing social order. Within the context of the absolutist centre, this led to the introduction and articulation of an alternative, or counter-tradition, with the existing State seen as an alien entity commanding duty and obligations, but not effective commitment. This tradition, merging with later developments—such as rural hostility to Parisian centrality, peasant reaction to revolutionary measures (grain con-fiscation, for instance)—became a central component of French traditions of protest and continued to inform and to structure the attitudes of the citizenry to the political framework and centre orders and symbols.

Related to these developments was a second important feature influencing protest: a tendency towards the political *de-autonomisation* of protesting elites such as the Huguenots and Jansenists. As noted, this development precluded the crystallisation of 'modernising elites' (often secondary elites) capable of articulating tradition in terms relevant to modern problems, interests and demands. The limited development of elites capable of modernizing tradition and transforming its contents, to bring them in line with the pressures and problems of a modernising collective; strengthened those social forces and elites who rejected the tradition '*tout court*'. While the formost expression of this trend was in the French Revolution itself, later developments such as the anachronism of French right-wing groups and the continual ambivalence of the French 'left' to the legacy of the Revolution, betray the continued problems of the centre in eliciting support for its fundamental social assumption.

Similar to the closure placed on the development of autonomous secondary elites, was the dissociation between State-building and cultural elites discussed above. This, too, proved to be a critical element for the subsequent path of protest. It engendered the particular dissonance between various cultural elites and the institutions of the State which prevades French historical development. From Richelieu's fear of café society as centres of subversion, to the University closures after May 1968, the mutual distrust between the State and the intelligentsia has continued to characterise the French social structure.[57] This hostility, a result of the only partial integration or incorporation of major groups of cultural elites into the centre, led to the crystallisation of major groups of protesting elites who, with limited commitment to the centre, continued to articulate alternative conceptions of the social order.

Another, no less important, element influencing the characteristics of French protest was the nature of Church–State relations during the course of historical development. The continuing autonomy of the Church as an articulator of orientations bearing on the political sphere (a characteristic structured by the particular relations between ecclesiastical authorities and State-building elites in the period of early modern nation formation), proved to be an important and constant element in the development of protest. It found expression both in the legitimation granted to right-wing political elites, and in the continuing anti-clericalism of republican and radical elites. Similarly, the refusal of the Church to accommodate itself to the norms of a secular/political community until relatively late in the stage of nation formation and centre crystallisation, lent added weight to the revolutionary elites' orientation against the centre (which, whatever its rhetoric, had reached a *modus vivendi* with a recalcitrant Church).

A similar influence of earlier traditions and elite structure on later developments was felt in the realm of political legitimation. For the distinction between centre and periphery which resulted from the dissociation between State-building and cultural elites continued to structure the relations between political elites and social groups. This relation was characterised by the construction of strong local networks of influence, power and prestige between contending groups of political and social elites articulating opposing models of collective solidarity and political legitimation. As a result, traditional right-wing political elites were able to elicit support and mobilisation in many areas and sectors of society by channeling traditional hostility to the centre.[58] Furthermore, the slow process of normative, educational and linguistic acculturation of the whole territorial populace, as exemplified by the problematic development of the secular educational system, continued to enable clerical elites to articulate their value orientations in rural areas as yet untouched by those values being formed in the urban centres.[59]

This feature was bound closely to the continual problems of national consolidation and the construction of collective identity which persisted into this century. The problematic nature of this construction lay, *inter alia*, in developments in the sphere of elite impingement (as structured by past traditions). The early separation of elites, for instance, led to a plurality of articulators of collective models—clerical elites of the Church, left-wing political elites, monarchists, cultural elites and social reformers such as the Fourierists and Saint Simonists—each articulating competing orientations towards the symbolic centre. Their continuing impingement on the social centre and on each other, and the lack of a framework of consensus for social and political interaction, engendered a continuing and particularly salient struggle over the definition of the symbolic dimensions of existence.

Furthermore, the propensity of the Revolution to sharpen certain rifts within the social structure intensified conflicts over modes of solidarity and identification in a number of realms. The early crystallisation of the geopolitical centre, autonomous and distinct from the territorial periphery, led to problems of cultural regionalism which continued throughout the nineteenth century. Similarly, the development of the political centre, with neither a break from Rome, on the one hand, nor, on the other, the integration of clerical elites into the State led to continuing secular/clerical tensions in society. These tensions were expressed through the continual conflicts and impingement between clerical and secular elites in nineteenth century France. They were manifest not only in the orientations articulated, but also in institution structures, networks of patronage, conflicting prestige criteria and *loci* of political power.[60] This split between the State and clerical elites, which widened during the post-revolutionary period, continued to divide society over fundamental issues of collective life, definition of the social order and notions of national identity and criteria for membership. Roles changed in the course of time, as did ideological positions, but the fundamental divisions remained, many of them rooted in the interpretation of and identification with the historical events which formed the nation-state.

Notes

1. M. Bloch, *Feudal Society*, London, Routledge and Kegan Paul, 1961.
2. P. Anderson, *Lineages of the Absolutist State*, London, New Left books, 1974.
3. See D. Bitton, *The French Nobility in Crisis 1560–1640*, Standford, Standford University Press, 1969; and F. Ford, *The Robe and the Sword*, New York, Harper and Row, 1953.
4. See S. Rokkan, 'Dimensions of State Formation and Action-Building: A Possible Paradigm for Research on Variations within Europe', in C. Tilly, (ed.), *The Formation of National States in Western Europe*, Princeton, Princeton University Press, 1975.
5. See Anderson, *Lineages*; Barrington Moore Jr., *Social Origins of Dictatorship and Democracy; Lord and Peasant in the making of the Modern World*, Boston, Beacon Press, 1966; W. Fischer and P. Lundgreen, 'The Recruitment and Training of Administrative and Technical Personnel', in C. Tilly, (ed.), *The Formation of Nation States*.
6. A. D. Lublinshaya, *French Absolutism: The Crucial Phase 1670–1679*, Cambridge, Cambridge University Press, 1968.
7. See Fischer and Lundgreen in C. Tilly, (ed.), *The Formation of Nation States*.
8. See Ford, *The Robe and the Sword*.
9. See Anderson, *Lineages*; and Barrington Moore Jr., *Origins*.
10. See Barrington Moore Jr., *Origins*.
11. For the relevant historical background to these developments, as well as to the institutional crystallisation of the absolutist centre see, in addition to the above, J. Russel Major, *Representative Institutions in Renaissance France, 1421–1559*, Madison, University of Wisconsin Press, 1960; J. H. M. Salmon, *Society in Crises, France in the Sixteenth Century*, London, E. Benn, 1975; P. Goubert, *Louis XIV and Twenty Million Frenchmen*, New York, Vintage Books, 1973; R. Bendix, *Kings Or People*, Berkeley, University of California Press, 1978; D. Buisseret, *Sully and the Growth of Centralized Government in France, 1598–1610*. London, 1968.
12. For studies of the humanists see R. Mandrou, *From Humanism to Science*, Middlesex, Penguin, 1978; L. Febvre and H. J. Martin, *The Coming of the Book*, London, NLB, 1976; N. O. Keohane, *Philosophy and the State in France*, Princeton, Princeton University Pess, 1980; D. Kelly, *The Beginnings of Ideology*, Cambridge, Harvard University Press, 1981; G. Skinner, *The Foundation of Modern Political Thought* (Vol. 2), Cambridge, Harvard University Press, 1978.
13. See S. N. Eisenstadt, *The Protestant Ethic and Modernization*, New York, Free Press, 1968; and more specifically, J. H. Franklin, *Constitutionalisation and Resistance in the Sixteenth Century*, New York, Penguin, 1969.
14. For two different aspects of this development see H. Luthey, *Banque Protestante en France*, Paris, 1961; and M. Waltzer, *The Revolution of the Saints*, Cambridge, Harvard University Press, 1965.
15. See N. Abercrombie, *The Origins of Jansenism in France*, Oxford, Oxford

Unversity Press, 1936; D. Van Klee, *The Jansenists and the Expulsion of the Jesuits from France*, New Haven, Yale University Press, 1973; L. Goldman, *The Hidden God*, London, Routledge and Kegan Paul, 1964.

16. See B. Groethysen, *The Bourgeoise, Catholicism vs. Capitalism in Eighteenth Century France*, London, The Cresent Press, 1968; F. Borkenau, *Der Ubergang von Feudalen zum Burgerlichen Weltbild: Studien zur Geschichter der Manufaturperiode*, Paris, 1934; as well as A. Burguiere, 'From Malthus to Max Weber; Related Marriage and the Spirit of Enterprise', in *Family and Society, Selections from Annales*, Foster and Ranum, (eds.), 2, Baltimore.

17. See especially, Waltzer, *The Revolution*; H. G. Koenigsberger, 'The Organization of Revolutionary Parties in France and Netherlands During the Sixteenth Century' in idem *Estates And Revolutions*, pp. 224–52, Ithaca, Cornell University Press, 1976; and Skinner, *Foundation*.

18. See T. Skocpol, *States and Social Revolutions*, Cambridge, Harvard University Press, 1979; H. Barber, *The Bourgeoisie in 18th Century France*, Princeton, Princeton University Press, 1955; Barrington Moore Jr., *Origins*; A. Goodwin, 'The Social and Economic and Political Attitudes of the French Nobility in the 18th Century', XII, International Congress of Historical Sciences, *Rapports*, 1.

19. Skocpol, *States*, p. 56.

20. See Barrington Moore, *Origins*; Anderson, *Lineages*; P. Birnbaum, 'States, Ideologies and Collective Action in Western Europe', *International Social Science Journal*, 32, p. 4, 1980.

21. See Skocpol, *States*, pp. 112–26; P. Goubert, *The Ancien Regime: French Society, 1600–1750*, London, Weidenfeld and Nicholson, 1975; C. Tilly, 'Food Supply and Public Order in Modern Europe' in Tilly, (ed.), *The Formation of Nation States*.

22. See S. N. Eisenstadt, *Revolution and the Transformation of Society*, New York, Free Press, 1976.

23. For theoretical perspectives see Eisenstadt, *Revolution*; and Skocpol, *States*. For historical background see G. Lefebvre, *The French Revolution*, 2 Vols., London, Routledge and Kegan Paul, 1962; A. Cobban, *A History of Modern France*, Vol. 1, Middlesex, Penguin, 1957; A. Soboul, *The French Revolution 1787–1789*, New York, Vintage Books, 1975; L. Hunt, *Politics, Culture and Class in the French Revolution*, Berkeley, University of California Press, 1984.

24. See Eisenstadt, *Revolution*, 1978; and R. Bendix, *Kings or People*, Berkeley, University of California Press, 1978.

25. For different aspects of this dynamic as well as strong centre orientations of modern movements of protest see E. Kamenka, *A World in Revolution*, Canberra, The Australian National University, 1970; 'The Concept of a Political Revolution' in C. J. Friedrich, *Revolution: Yearbook of the American Society for Political and Legal Philosophoy*, Nomos 8, N. J., Atherton, 1967; and G. Lichtheim, *The Origins of Socialism*, London, Weidenfeld and Nicholson, 1968.

26. The predominance of different legal occupational groups, for example, as cultural and political elite was one of the distinctive characteristics of French society during this period. See T. Zeldin *France 1848–1945*, Vol. 1, Oxford, Clarendon Press, 1979.

27. See Zeldin, *France*; and Soltau, *French Political Thought in the Nineteenth Century*, New York, Russel and Russell, 1959.

28. See Skocpol, *States*, pp. 178–205.

29. See Skocpol, *States*.

30. For different aspects of this restructuring see G. Dupeux, *French Society 1789–1970*, London, Methuen, 1976; A Cobban *op. cit*. Vol. 2, 1957; G. Morazes, *The Triumph of the Middle Classes*, Garden City, Doubleday Co., 1968.

31. This re-orientation in the fundamental symbolic assumptions of the centre was felt even in the Restoration of Louis XVIII which, while granting little to the principles of parliamentary democracy, could not ignore the fundamental symbolic changes in principles of legitimation articulated during the Revolution. (Hence, for example, the contradictory nature of the Charter of 1814.) See Cobban, *A History*. pp. 71–81.

32. For the continuing saliency of traditional orientations among the peasantry as an example of this dynamic see E. Weber, *Peasants Into Frenchmen*, Stanford, Stanford University Press, 1976. For a study of the different rightist groups in post-revolutionary France, see R. Remond, *The Right-Wing in France from 1815 to de Gaulle*, Philadelphia, University of Pennsylvania Press, 1968.

33. For example, the very modernisation of government bureaucratic structure, the creation of '*La France Functionelle*' of civil and military functionaries, of a legislative system and organs all symbolised the overthrow of absolutism, but, at the same time, also instituted both greater areas of centre penetration of the periphery and, *inter alia*, of periphery response, a dynamic which reflected the general re-orientation in the nature of centre–periphery relations.

34. For important and comparative insights into the role of eighteenth century social conflicts as structuring the symbolic boundaries of collective life, see S. M. Lipset, 'Radicalism or Reformism: The Sources of Working Class Politics', Presidential Address presented at the American Political Science Association Annual Meetings, September 2, 1982, Denver.

35. See R. Cobb, *The Police and the People: French Popular Protest, 1789–1920*. New York, 1970; Cobban, *A History*; E. Shorter and C. Tilly, *Strikes in France, 1830–1968*, London, Cambridge University Press, 1974; S. Elwitt, *The Making of the Third Republic*, Baton Rouge, Louisiana State University Press, 1975; P. Amman, *Revolution and Mass Democracy*, Princeton, Princeton University Press, 1975; B. Moss, *Origins of the French Labor Movement 1830–1914*, Berkeley, University of California Press, 1976.

36. See, for example, V. Lorwin, *The French Labor Movement*, Cambridge, Harvard University Press, 1954; Elwitt, *The Making of the Third Republic*.

37. See Amman, *Revolution and Mass Democracy*.

38. For the 'mediation' of those orientations by territorial, cultural and regional loyalties, see especially T. Zeldin, *France 1848–1945* Ambition Love and Politics, 2 Vols, Oxford, Oxford University Press, 1973.

39. See Remond, *The Right-Wing*.

40. See E. Weber, *The Nationalist Revival in France*, Berkeley, University of California Press, 1978.

41. For literature on revolutionary elites see Amman, *Revolution*; Lorwin, *The French Labor Movement*; R. Price, *The French Second Republic, A Social History*, London, Batsford, 1972; R. Ridley, *Revolutionary Syndicalism in France*, Cambridge, Harvard University Press, 1970; C. Tilly, *From Mobilisation to Revolution*, Reading, Addison-Wesley Publishing Co., 1976; Moss, *Origin*.

42. See P. Birnbaum, 'States, ideologies and collective action in Western Europe', *International Social Science Journal*, 2, No. 4, 1980, pp. 671–86.

43. For studies of republican elites, see P. Bertocci, *Jules Simon: Republican Anti-Clericalism and Cultural Politics in France 1848–1886*, Columbia University of Missouri Press, 1978; Elwitt, *The Making*; L. Greenberg, *Sisters of Liberty, Marseille, Lyon, Paris and the Reaction to a Centralized State*, Cambridge, Harvard University Press, 1971. For studies of these elites outside the political context, see Zeldin, *Ambition, Love and Politics*.

44. For different aspects of Utopian and Reformist Thought, see G. Ionescu, *The Political Thought of Henri Saint Simon*, London, 1976; L. A. Loubere, *Louis Blanc: His Life and Historical Contribution to the Rise of French Jacobian Socialism*, Evanston, Northwestern University Press, 1961; H. Lubac, *The Un-Marxian Socialist: A Study of Proudhorn*, New York, Sheed and Ward, 1948; F. Manuel, *Utopian Thought in the Western World*, Oxford, Oxford University Press, 1979; N. Riasanovsky, *The Teaching of Charles Fourier*, Berkeley, University of California Press, 1969; A. Ritter, *The Political Thought of Pierre-Joseph Proudhorn*, Princeton, Princeton University Press, 1969; T. Zeldin, *The Educational Ideas of Charles Fourier*, London, F. Cass, 1969.

45. There are fine bibliographies on the Ultracists, Legitimists and Orleanists in Remond, *The Right-Wing*, pp. 427–32.

46. See J. M. Thompson, *Louis Napoleon and the Second Empire*, Oxford, B. Blackwell, 1954; T. Zeldin, *The Political System of Napoleon III*, London, Macmillan, 1958.

47. For the joint action of socialists and republicans, see R. Anderson, *op.cit.*, 1977; Elwitt, *The Making of the Third Republic*.

48. See S. Hoffman, *In Search of France: The Economy, Society and Political System in the Twentieth Century*, New York, Harper and Row, 1965.

49. This was exemplified in the constitution of the Third Republic, the longest lasting and briefest of French constitutions. Originally conceived as temporary, it provided a compromise between monarchists and republicans. Its three laws and thirty-four articles were composed by members of different parties and lacked a proclamation of purpose or fundamental rights. This lacuna paradoxically made for its longevity, as the stability of

the regime rested on the flexibility allowed by the constitution. As Stanley Hofman has pointed out: 'The genuis of the Third Republic was the devising of an institutional set-up effectively adapted to French society . . . where the role of the State was kept strictly limited . . . an instrument, not a master', Hoffman, *In Search of France*, p. 14.

50. See D. Brogan, *The Development of Modern France 1870–1939*, London, H. Hamilton, 1967; Chapman, *The Third Republic of France. The First Phase 1871–1894*, London, Macmillan 1962; Elwitt, *The Making*.

51. See R. Anderson, *France 1870–1914: Politics and Society*, London, Routledge and Kegan Paul, 1977; Chapman, *The Third Republic of France*.

52. For different aspects of this conflict, see Soltau, *French Political Thought*; and especially T. Zeldin, (ed.), *Conflicts in French Society*, London, G. Allen and Unwin, 1971. For the continuity of these conflicts see J. McManners, *Church and State in France 1870–1914*, London, SPCK, 1972.

53. See K. Auspitz, *The Radical Bourgeoisie: The Ligue de l'Enseignement and the Origins of the Third Republic*, Cambridge, Cambridge University Press, 1982.

54. For different aspects of French modernisation, see R. E. Cameron, *France and the Economic Development of Europe 1800–1914*, Princeton, Princeton University Press, 1961; W. O. Henderson, *The Industrial Revolution on the Continent, Germany, France and Russia, 1800*–1914, London, F. Cass, 1961; A. L. Dunham, *The Industrial Revolution in France*, New York, Exposition Press, 1955; J. Marczewski, 'The take-off hypothesis and the French experience', in W. W. Rostow, *The Economics of Take-Off into Sustained Growth*, London, Macmillan, 1968, pp. 119–38.

55. For many of the following insights, I am indebted to V. Wright, see his paper 'Fragmentation and Cohesion in the Nation-State, France 1870–1871' at the European Science Foundation Seminar on *The Construction and Reconstruction of Centre-Periphery Relations in Europe*, Jerusalem, 28/5–1/6/1984.

56. Andre Sigfrieds' 'geographic determinism', especially as modified and sophisticated by modern geographers, points to many continuities between historical and modern France. See his *Tableau Politique de la France de l'Ouest sous la IIIe Republique*. Paris, 1964.

57. J. Leclant, 'Coffee and Cafes in Paris 1644–1693', in R. Forster and O. Ranum, eds., *Food and Drink in History, Selections from the Annales*. 5, p. 91.

58. See A. D. Tudesq, *Les Grands Notables en France 1840–1849*, Paris, 1964, pp. 130–236.

59. See Weber, *Peasants*.

60. Much of this awareness has indeed evolved from the plethora of regional studies conducted over the last two decades and indeed from the sophisticated electoral sociology developed in France and centred around the Fondation Nationale des Sciences Politiques.

3 Centre formation and political participation in Spain and Italy: an interpretation of Southern European politics

Luis Roniger

In search of a 'deep structure'

In the early 1980's, the so-called Mediterranean societies of Europe, namely Portugal, Spain, Italy, Greece, Cyprus and Malta exhibited a formal political physiognomy that closely resembled that of other Western European states. Constitutionally, most were parliamentary democracies with some form of representational institutions and competing party systems. They held contested elections and generally maintained unrestricted party activities. Beyond this formal level, however, there were fundamental social and political differences between the Mediterranean area and most other Western European settings. A cursory examination indicates, for instance, that Portugal, Spain, and Greece, after years, in the first two cases, decades, of authoritarian rule, only recently became parliamentary democracies; that the political systems of nations such as Italy or Cyprus have lacked widespread legitimacy among broad sectors of their own populations, leading, as in the case of Cyprus, to separatist trends in their political structuring; that the political centres of several of these societies have not commanded a strong commitment, whether among parts of their consitutive elites or among the broader strata; and that these have been the main regions in Western Europe where corporatism and clientelism have flourished and remained salient to date.

These featrues—authoritarianism, contested legitimacy, partial commitment, corporatism, and clientelism, which have characterized these polities for long periods, suggest that within the common tradition of Western Europe these nations are to some extent distinct in the character of their political centres, centre–periphery relations, and articulation and incorporation of demands and protest.

For many years scholars have been aware that the so called Mediterranean polities evolved somehow differently.[1] Still these polities were almost systematically excluded from comparative political studies on Western Europe. Recently, political scientists increasingly emphasize that the parallel and similar developments in many aspects of the Mediterranean political systems as well as in their patterns of social and economic development, warrant systematic study.[2] Still, few attempts have been made to analyse whether impressions are correct and there indeed has been some 'deep structure' (to paraphrase Claude Levi-Strauss)[3] in the structuring of Mediterranean polities in the nineteenth and twentieth centuries. This will be the major aim of this article, namely to analyse from a comparative perspective major processes of centre formation and political participation in Southern European polities. For this purpose, I shall focus on two highly dissimilar cases: Spain, a nation-state with a pronounced (at least symbolic) reliance on its imperial past and Italy, a nation-state comprised of multiple regional centres which crystallised in the mid-nineteenth century.

The configuration of modern Spanish and Italian political centres

The polycentric nature of European society was replicated both in Spain and Italy in the existence of different regional, cultural and political cleavages. These scissions were conducive to a peculiar dynamic of configuration of political centres and political struggle and in each country assumed a singular path of development. We shall begin by looking at the respective processes of configuration of political centres of each society.[4]

Spain

Spain had a tradition of a strong imperial centre, which evolved during the *reconquista* and the subsequent conquest of American lands and influx of wealth. Since the completion, in the late fifteenth century, of the process of reconquering the lands that were to become Spain, and the discovery and conquest of the American territories, the Spanish centre embodied the ideal of a universal Catholic monarchy colonizing and converting the world. With its developed bureaucracy, strong army, and the close relationship of its quest for power with a sense of mission, the monarchy succeeded in breaking up the political strength of the nobility at an early stage. It did, however, encourage, or at least did not hamper, the aristocracy's attempts to monopolise basic sources of livelihood such as lands in Southern Spain or commerce with the

Latin American colonies. The centre weakened, and entered a period of decay in the seventeenth century. Nevertheless, it continued to affect the periphery with bureaucratic demands of political order and taxation. Even if symbolically strong, it in fact conducted policies of encapsulation and adaptive relations with upper strata in the periphery, recognizing the power domains of those local and regional elites which acknowledged the primacy of the centre. It also implemented strong extractive policies in the more active poles of development, as in nineteenth century Cataluña.

The short-lived attempts of the Bourbon rulers to reshape the policies of national integration in the late eighteenth century, the subsequent French occupation, and the war of liberation in the early nineteenth century, led to fundamental changes in the centre's legitimisation criteria. Most Latin American colonies had been lost by the 1830's. Struggles broke out among elite sectors (Royalists versus Carlists, for example) in bids to take over power. Liberalist political institutions were formally established, with intermittent periods of unrest, on the one hand, and centralisation and order, on the other. The bases of political legitimacy changed from autocratic kingship to popularly sanctioned and constitutionally established authority. Nevertheless, kingship remained a strong symbol of legitimacy and of representation of Spanish unity. Accordingly the King was expected to play a central role as the authoritative mediator of political struggles, mainly as a source of authority and unity, rather than as a constructor of the basic rules of political game.[5]

Italy

In Italy there were multiple centres and a tradition of communal civility. Through the Middle Ages and the Renaissance, Italy was an agglomerate of republics, city-states, papal dominions duchies, and smaller power domains. Until the nineteenth century, large areas were ruled by foreign powers. Austria dominated Istria, Venetia and Lombardy and was influential in the duchies of Parma, Modena and Toscana, as well as in the Papal states and in the Bourbon Kingdom of the Two Sicilies. Piedmont and the Kingdom of Sardinia remained a largely French-inspired regime. The building of an unitary centre was a relatively late process, undertaken in the mid-nineteenth century by such different intellectual and political forces as the Liberals and the Republicans, headed by the House of Savoja. These forces articulated orientations towards independence from the foreign rulers that had dominated Italy for centuries. The political centre was created in the 1860's out of one of the pre-existing centres, with the support of the Piedmontese political class. Such a centre succeeded in becoming the focus for presentation of demands and participation of regional leaderships and managed to become a workable, enduring framework, in spite of rapid changes in its structure—from monarchy and parliamentary democracy to fascism, and later to republican forms—and in spite of an apparent lack of broadly active commitment after its initial period of formation.

At first glance, the modes of configuration of these two political centres differ widely from one another and therefore, the societies' political dynamics can be explained, on one level, as much of the literature has attempted, in terms of the particular characteristics of the concrete social and political forces that shaped their contours.[6] I shall try to find out, however, whether beyond the concrete peculiarities of each setting both political systems faced, in different, but yet similar ways, dilemmas of political participation and shared various patterns of resolution of struggles and incorporation of demands within their polities.

This search for disparate paths and common patterns can be pursued hereafter by analysing two innovative, and therefore 'decisive', periods of modern state formation in these societies: the period of 1873–1936 from the First Republic to the defeat of the Second Republic in Spain, during which Spaniards attempted to establish new institutions and workable forms of political articulation; and the initial period of configuration of the 'unitary' state in Italy (1860–1922).

Processes of state configuration: Spain in the 'Republic-Restoration-Republic' period (1873–1936)

The period between the establishment of the short-lived First Republic in 1873 and the defeat of the Republican forces in 1936 was one of religious-ideological cleavages and of regional, cultural and class conflicts. Fragmentation of parties and political movements was rampant; the centre was increasingly too weak to face them; too many exclusive interests appeared and the parliamentary system—which was manipulated by the executive and political forces it temporarily supported—could not contain them. Secular forces opposed clerical ones; nationalist organisations faced new radical ones; and the Carlists split. Later, the republicans faced the socialists; moderate republicans opposed leftist republicans; regionalists were divided on the question of the use of force; the anarchists failed to cooperate with the communists; the Catholics were divided; liberal parties and offshoots proliferated. Coalitions were unstable and splits common. There was a trend among parties and movements to atomize on ideological issues and to concede special importance to personalistic questions. There was a low level of formalisation and organisation of parties. Conflict and violence were not contained within an institutional framework and struggles were mainly recurrent confrontations between forces that lacked a common basis for consensual interaction. Spaniards were accordingly reported to be 'ungovernable' and to move intermittently from 'passionate' participation in politics to apathy. A low degree of compromise was found among political forces, both on the central and more local levels. Such trends were particularly evident in the 1931–36 period, with which we deal in some detail below.

The interlude of Primo-de-Riviera's dictatorship (1923–1930, after the so-called Bolshevist trienium), came to an end with the narrowing of his base of support during the world economic depression and the increasingly active expressions of reproval of intellectual circles, Catalonian autonomists, and sectors of the working classes. The King (Alfonso XIII) opted to call for municipal elections which, though fraudulent and based on the manipulation of votes by *caciques* (local and regional bosses) and the pre-arranged outcome of electoral results in local communities, still provided evidence of the narrow support for the monarchical forces in the main cities. These results, interpreted as the failure to amass strong 'moral support', precipitated the abdication of the king and delivering political power—on the advice of the principal army generals—into the hands of a surprised Republican committee, thereby initiating a three-year Republican rule.

Unstable governments replaced one another, each governing for an average of three and a half months. Coalitions both within and outside the centre divided and regrouped, and over thirty parties and political movements contested for power, with little regard for constitutional forms. Major political groups, once outside the government, worked against ruling forces by whatever means were at their disposal. Such a pattern of political struggle was a recurrent feature of this period, as exemplified in the following instances. First, General Sansurjo—probably the main social actor behind Alfonso XIII's abdication of power in favour of the Republicans—attempted, only fourteen months after this abdication, to take power himself in a typical *pronunciamiento*. Similarly, in 1934, after participating in the government for two years, the Socialist Party revolted against the current powerholders, and the government decided to repress the Asturias revolt with force, using

Moorish and foreign legionary troops. In 1936, after their success in the parliamentary elections, the Republicans and the Socialist forces of Largo Cabellero failed to collaborate in establishing a common government. These and other events of the period occurred within a framework of polarisation and increased violence between ideological groups (such as the Socialists and the Communist youth, on the one hand, and the Catholic CEDA, on the other); between partisans of separatism and autonomy for the peripheral regions, on the one hand, and of centralisation and unity, on the other; and between different social classes. The violent and noncoalescing multiple character of political confrontations, which the international forces that impinged on the Spanish scene in those years did nothing to deter, finally erupted in the Spanish Civil War. Such confrontations were ultimately muted during the subsequent highly-centralised and authoritarian-corporatist Franquist rule.

Processes of state configuration: the initial period of the establishment of the unitary state in Italy (1860–1922)

The unification was effected under the motto of unity, independence, and freedom (interpreted in liberal terms of economic development). The return to a glorious ancient past which could provide common links of language and culture was as well a major symbolic promise held up by the main forces behind the unification: the Piedmontese king, the army, and small intellectual circles, mostly of northern middle- and upper-class romantics, backed by the France of Napoleon III. Attempts to mobilize locally-oriented peasants were insubstantial and in the so-called 'unitarian' centralised State that followed the incorporation of the Italian *Mezzogiorno* (Southern part of the peninsula), power remained in the hands of the liberal moderates, with the support of more radical elements, such as Giuseppe Mazzini's Republicans. Traditional aristocratic circles and the upper middle classes retained influence in the new state. The political centre indeed was based on a compromise between the liberal middle class, mainly of Northern entrepreneurs and professionals, and the Southern aristocracy mainly of landed elites. Notwithstanding, or perhaps as a result of the fact that the state adopted a centralised character to the detriment of regional autonomy and relied on delegated powerholders such as bureaucrats instead of on elected administrative bodies, it was unable to incorporate effectively broader strata and peripheral areas. The Southern peasants, for instance, were left untouched by the construction of a unitary state, and while they resented the economic consequences of the policies implemented by the state, they remained under the strong influence of anti-unitarian and conservative forces, such as the traditional supporters of the former Bourbon rulers and the local clergy. These were the social actors that instigated the peasants against the new central authorities.

Formally, the legal apparatus of the Kingdom of Piedmonte and Sardinia—the Statuto Albertino—became the central law of the state, with strong powers delegated to the King. It was modelled on the Napoleonic state, with the centre controlling the periphery through appointed *prefetti*, officials charged with the sum of power in the locality.

Within the parliamentary scene, the existence of still 'uncompleted national tasks', such as the incorporation of Rome and the Veneto region in the first decade of independence, provided a common denominator for broad coalitions between political forces, known as the 'right' and the 'left', and within the latter, between Mazzini's Republicans and Depreti's Moderates. The main dividing line between political forces in those years and for some decades to come was the demand of some of the sectors that popular action be taken towards liberating Rome. This of course affected the temporal position of the Pope. It was also resented by one of the main external supporters of the new state (France) and in fact triggered the 'non expedit' policy (1874) of the Vatican against the participation of Roman Catholics in the political life of the secular state, which thereby reduced the state's bases of support until the twentieth century.

The economic processes that the *Mezzogiorno* underwent soon led to an outbreak of peasant revolts and strikes, mainly against work conditions and economic backwardness. Though protest was mostly local, it affected a wide geographic area, as it had the covert encouragement of anti-unitarian forces. Sometimes, this protest merged with *brigantaggio* (bandit) raids, which expressed rejection of the state's administrative and legal apparatus. The state dealt with these revolts by means of military repression and the courts, a policy which in fact did not arouse significant debate among the political forces at the centre. The state dismissed any incorporation of demands or cooptation of participants, probably due to the combined effects of the physical distance of the revolts from the central regions, the lack of a unified and articulated leadership among the revolters, the disarticulated demands expressed, and the loss of external support once these demands became more radical and clearly social in character. The Southern upper strata at first resented some of the economic measures taken by the national state, such as the abolition of protectionist regional barriers or the creation of a wide national communication system. However, they benefitted from the sale of ecclesiastic lands that strengthened the *latifondisti*'s hold in the Southern *Mezzogiorno*. In the long term, these social forces acceded to power, along with the intellectual circles who were critical of the Northern-based coalition of the 'right' (1860–76). Indeed, they became part of the ruling state coalitions and obtained recognition of their power domains which nonetheless were incorporated into the national state. At the same time, they increasingly penetrated the state's administrative and military machinery.

Following the completion of the national unity, the state attempted to incorporate broader strata through widening the educational system, expanding patronage and job opportunities in the civil bureacracy, and socialising army conscripts in an army led by officers of upper-aristrocratic and middle-class origins. Repression was the main mode of response to social demands until the late 1880's and early 1890's, when reforms were adopted, seemingly to allow for the smooth incorporation of the urban working classes into the political system. While these reforms enlarged electoral participation and the number of elective offices on the municipal and provincial levels, they confirmed the prominent position of the *prefetto* and retained the use of public security laws against labour organisations as the state's predominant instruments for controlling social forces. A second policy for attaining wide support and consensus was attempted through Italy's involvement in imperialistic enterprises since 1896.

Attempts to rely entirely on narrower coalitions, such as military and political forces grouped around the King during the 1897–1900 period, to forcefully repress workers' demands and protest failed. These coalitions were replaced by liberal coalitions, whose strategy aimed at incorporating the lower strata into multiclass political organisations participating in a policy of accommodation. This strategy was maintained until 1913, when the King, supported by narrow urban groups of mainly disaffected intellectuals and extra-parliamentary factors, forced a change in policy and powerholders. This development, together with the implementation of an interventionist international war policy—neither of which elicited wide support, and only the reluctant and tenuous agreement of active political forces—precipitated a series of developments that ultimately led to the King's call *chiamata* to Mussolini to take power in 1922. The rise of fascism to power was facilitated by the fragmentation and internal cleavages of parliamentary political forces such as the Catholics and the Socialists. These forces were interested in maintaining their clientelistic networks and stood by their sectarian ideological tenets, failing to collaborate in resisting fascism from entering the parliament and forming a government which managed to obtain emergency powers.

Singularities and common paths

A first look at these periods in the political history of Spain and Italy, as well as analyses of later periods, indicates that Spanish and Italian political forces participated differently in the formation and restructuring of political centres. First of all, each modelled their access to power differently. In Spain, such traits as the activism of political forces, orientations of elites and sub-elites to the seizure of power and the transformation of socio-political order, the mushrooming of political efforts, and exclusivism rather than compromise and cooptation in confronting oppositions were prominent. Consequently, when some of the active elites could not afford to accede to power they often opted for emigration from the country, expecting to return only to enter central positions of government.[7] In Italy, elites and sub-elites were motivated to participate in the political centre and to compromise with each other, rather than to oppose contrary policies by challenging the whole political system and taking recourse to armed revolts as in Spain. Pragmatism was the rule in elite interaction.[8]

Second, the differences in elite interaction and struggle reflected the crystallisation of distinct patterns of interaction between elites and masses. While in Spain the ruling class frequently resorted to exclusivism in relation to sectors of society such as the peasantry, the ruling elites in Italy had to work out the bases of legitimacy and often had to use forms of cooptation to broaden their bases of support. In Italy cooptation did not preclude repression, especially of the lower classes, who nevertheless were enfranchised within a relatively short period after the establishment of the State, as mass parties appeared and electoral contests developed. Thus, in Italy, bases of support and participation were comparatively broad and tended to be widened. (Autocratic attempts by the King and his supporters to limit the participatory nature of the political system and to rely on extra-parliamentary forces failed, save when these forces succeeded in replacing the King as a source of authority and legitimacy, later on, during the fascist period.)

Third, the patterns of elite interaction and struggle took place within different forms of centre–periphery relations and different forms of control and tolerance of regionalism, in each case. Spain had greater capacity than Italy to penetrate the least mobilised areas of agrarian capitalism (parts of Andalusia and Extremadura in Spain, and Western Sicily in Italy). This was due to the Spanish centre's combined use of *caciquismo* and the Guardia Civil corps (created in 1843); both instruments of rule precluded the emergence of local and regional independent brokers like the Western Sicilian *mafiosi*.[9] In both countries regional identities crystallised and lack of commitment to the centre existed on the part of broad sectors in these regions. But drives towards separatism were especially pronounced in Spain, where regional linguistic and cultural differences coalesced with primordial identities.[10]

The regional location of the centres was also of paramount significance in structuring the different forms of centre–periphery relations in each case. In Spain, the political centre was located in a region which was of minor economic significance. Being organisationally weak and financially indebted, such a political centre was driven to implement extractive policies in the richer periphery; these policies provided the centre with those means of control needed to subdue periphery interests to its own. In contrast, the Italian political centre, by virtue of its location and support in the more developed areas of the peninsula, did not have to penetrate the Southern regions with strong extractive policies. On the contrary, it could afford to implement policies of redistribution of resources and to grant a relatively non-separatist autonomy to various regions within the country.[11]

The attitude of the Catholic Church and its placement in relation to the secular state in each of the countries studied here was central to the state's position in articulating the national community and its identities. In Spain, the Church was traditionally a basic component of the centre. It provided many of the symbols and images for the establishment of social and political order, and accepted a certain segregation of spheres, according to which the political centre was recognised as the ultimate arbiter in temporal matters within Spain and its colonies, in return for supporting the Church in its universal moral mission and international position. At the same time, the participation of the Church and its influence in the Spanish political centre were not negligible. It remained at the heart of political struggles and conflicts during the nineteenth and twentieth centuries, especially as the ruling coalitions dissociated themselves from traditional interests and commitments, as for example, during the Second Republic.

In Italy, the Church resented the creation of a secular centre and the establishment of its capital in Rome, which was traditionally the centre of Catholicism. For the Church, the unification of Italy meant a loss of prominence in international contacts with the main European powers, and a loss of its temporal power over territories of which only the

Vatican remained. Accordingly, the Church assumed the role of 'counter-centre', commanding the commitment of wide sectors of the population, which, in the 1880's, were asked to refrain from political participation. The Church collaborated politically, if not socially, with secessionist movements such as the Southern *brigantaggio* and the peasant revolts of the late nineteenth century. Later on, it actively participated as a political force in shaping the centre, expressing its recognition of the boundaries of the Italian State and nation, fostering the constitution of political organisations (such as the Partito Populare Italiano of don Luigi Sturzo) and labour unions, and becoming related to power through the leadership of the Christian Democratic Party.

Thus far, the singular character of each of the cases under consideration was singled out. It has been indicated that in Spain, political cleavages often assumed territorial connotations, and the political centre—located in an economically backward region—implemented extractive policies; there, workable regimes fully endorsed policies of centralisation (as exemplified since the late 1930's by such ideologically distinct regimes as that of Franco and the subsequent democracy); there, too, protest and conflict, being oriented to the political centre, adopted extreme and often tragic connotations.

By contrast, in Italy, political cleavages did not have such territorial significance; national participation originated in the economically advanced areas of the North; conflicts erupted on a village-to-village level, embracing forces which identified with the political actors confronting each other on the national level; there, while the Church acted initially as a 'counter-centre', in a relatively short period, the central political forces adopted more pragmatic forms of mutual accommodation, ultimately remaining committed to participation in the political centre.[22]

Beyond such singularities, idiosyncratic to each case, modern Spanish and Italian political systems have shared several traits which were fundamental in patterning political participation and struggle there. Prominent among them are the pervasiveness of deep social, regional, cultural and political cleavages; the force of enduring social hierarchies in general and of traditionally oriented elites in particular; and a continuously developing tension between exclusive criteria limiting social and political participation, on the one hand, and, on the other, manifest pressures to broaden such participation.

Connected to the above cleavages and tensions, modern Spanish and Italain polities have faced demands that concerned not only technical and instrumental (e.g., redistributive) rules but on the contrary, these demands often were connected and oriented to fundamental and still contested issues, such as the legitimacy that might turn the arrangements of distribution of power in society into a recognised and meaningful system, or the issue of the forms in which social, regional and other primordial identities might be articulated within a commonly agreed collective identity. Paradoxical as it may seem at first, these characteristics developed both in the political systems of Spain, with its imperial past, and in that of Italy, which crystallised much later in the mid-nineteenth century.

In both countries, the above demands have conditioned the nature of the political game, first and foremost in the sense that actual political arrangements and, as a consequence, the political realm itself, were perceived to be merely the result of a correlation of forces, and therefore devoid of those very aspects of 'centrality' associated with the socio-political centre. The result was a relatively low degree of commitment towards the political centres. This, in turn, led to a tendency among actors at the political centres to be oriented by exclusive or coopting policies, but in both instances, as well as in the more common situation of a combination of such policies, to be rather unresponsive to needs and tensions in society, except when these were advanced by forceful actions and/or by the activities of political brokers, mediators and social forces already at the *loci* of power or closely related with those in power.

These characteristics also indicate a peculiar dynamics of efforts to demobilise social forces, to centralise political and administrative decisions, and to mediate access to *loci* of power and markets; all these together with a tendency—more marked in Spain than in Italy—of political confrontations to become totalistic endeavours, oriented towards restructuring and redefining all the contours of socio-political life.

Thus, during most of the nineteenth and twentieth centuries, political actors in these societies granted legitimacy to rulers on conditional partisan terms; a low degree of commitment was expressed to actual political arrangements; and a plurality of forces and elites contested for power in forms that often undermined or affected the very legal foundations of the state.

These traits, found both in modern Spain and Italy as reflected in the processes of centre formation and reconstruction analysed above, condense and express a peculiar outlook on political struggle and participation which was typical of political actors in these societies.

In the first place, by granting legitimacy to rulers only on strictly conditional terms, political actors in these societies seem to have conceived that a basic distinction existed between their ideal conception of a centre and the actual political order projected by the organs of the state. In a sense, this epitomised the basic distinction, typical of Western Europe, between the law in its ideal and universalistic aspects (natural or Roman) and the state which attempts, with varying degrees of success, to be recognized as the interpretator and embodiment of the law.[13]

Second, conceptions of a natural order and law often were articulated by many competing forces and elites, a trend exacerbated by the regional and social cleavages of these societies: many sub-centres emerged; strong regional differences and identities crystallised; and territorial kinship and fragmented occupational units existed, which contributed—within the framework of the indicated institutional propensities—to the particular dynamics of centre building and political struggle. On a 'deeper' value level, these struggles were reinforced by the mutual impingement of Church and State, that is of institutions supposedly engaged respectively, in spiritual and mundane endeavours, and carrying other-worldly and this-worldly messages, but in fact impinging on each other and contesting to become foci of symbolic articulation of wide identities.

Third, political struggles seemed to have expressed a basic indeterminancy between the projection of conceptions of the social order as given, thus predicating a lack of participation in the routine shaping of the society, along with traditions of autonomous access to socio-political centres and of activism, sporadically expressed by disarticulated social movements. In the articulation of both conceptions, an emphasis has been placed on mediation of access of groups and strata both to the mundane and the transcendental orders (by such bodies as the Church and political powers and powerful individuals).

Fourth, the processes of centre building and political struggle revolved not only around procedural matters but mainly around two interconnected issues. One was the definition of the exact content of the common identity, over which political sectors and social forces disagreed, in addition to often being divided over the concrete relation which should be maintained between cultural, primordial, and civic identities. The other was the issue of the degree of legitimacy granted to the political system in terms of specifying which social and political forces are to be given access to or to be excluded from the *loci* of political authority, and in terms of the existence of, or failure to develop, workable institutional channels for settling the disagreements on these issues.

These institutional propensities were worked out in Southern Europe through the activities, struggles and alliances of social forces and elites, whose actions were modelled and/or constrained by perceptions of the 'proper' structuring of the socio-political order, which at the same time were crystallised and modified by these elites. It is therefore necessary to analyse in greater detail the forms in which the main social actors and political entrepreneurs participated in shaping the political realm in Spain and Italy.

Elites, the conception of the State and participation in the political realm

In the modern Southern Europe settings analysed here, the distinction between the conception of an ideal, transcendent natural order and the imperfection of the actual socio-political order was reflected in a weak institutional connection between fundamental (religiously-based) conceptions of order, on the one hand, and on the other, the realities of the state and state organs embodying this order. As mentioned above, this distinction was reflected also in the low degree of commitment to the political centre among broader strata both in Italy and Spain, in the latter despite the ideal image of a strong authoritative centre that remained widely accepted among Spaniards.

In Spain, the transition to a modern basis of legitimacy following the Napoleonic invasion and changes in the character of the centre and its elites, strengthened the existing conception that actual socio-political arrangements resulted from a relation between forces and, therefore, constituted a focus for continuous struggles around issues of incumbency, representation, and access to foci of decision-making. Nevertheless, the search for realisation of a wide (natural, broader, etc.) social order was directed at a centre. This was evident in the existence of competing elites and counter-elites attempting to articulate conceptions of natural law and order through struggles and competition for access to the political centre or their attempts to take it over. It was evident also in the demands presented by movements of protest such as the anarchists and the workers movement. These movements expressed their demands in a totalistic universalistic mode, even though structurally, they were divided along narrow regional lines of organisation, and accordingly faced serious problems in concerting common actions on a broad inter-regional and ideological basis.

In Italy, the creation of a national centre through active struggle against alien military forces and against the opposition of local aristocratic forces and the Church, initially led supporters of the secular state to believe it was widely accepted. However, this centre soon lost its appeal as a focus of national identity, as many of its supporters became disillusioned, and wide sectors of the population began to seek representation of the social order around the Church and its institutions. After Unification had been accomplished, the secular forces which had participated in it failed to articulate wider orientations as an alternative to the deep-rooted Catholic ones. Secular conceptions remained restricted to small elite circles, until the emergence of the Socialist movement at the beginning of the twentieth century and the fascist movement in the 1920's–1940's. The Demochristian governments of the post-war period on their part were linked to the Church as symbolic centre, and therefore faced severe problems in their attempts to constitute a focus of identification as major carriers of conceptions of a broad societal order, even if on a pragmatic level they succeeded in retaining power.

These perceptions of the nature of the socio-political realm also influenced the modes of participation of the principal political actors in this sphere of interaction. In Spain, the elites were oriented to transforming the socio-political order through political, 'secular', activities, and impinged on the weak centre during the crisis of authority and changes in the principles of legitimacy that occurred during the Napoleonic invasion in the early nineteenth century. Their liberal orientations, however, were considered alien to the basic nature of the centre, it was easy for other elites to gather forces to keep control of the state. Later, the Liberal parties entered the ruling coalition, but only after they had renounced radicalism and their links of solidarity with social strata like the urban plebians, whose actions had brought them political centrality.

In Italy, the relatively late formation of a secular state allowed the central elites within a few decades to overcome the Church's opposition to the demand for legitimacy required by the movement for the *Unity*. The original opposition lent a strong anti-Church sentiment to the struggle of the secular liberal elites, while the emergence of worker movements and syndicalist activity led the Church to adopt a pragmatic view and to collaborate in the building and functioning of the political centre.[14]

In Spain, the central elites and the political forces related to them have remained oriented towards the centre and towards the performance of bureaucratic administrative functions as a source of prestige and power to a larger extent than in Italy. In the latter, the image of the political centre has not been so highly valued and the bureacracy has played a less central role in the control of access to power, even if it has been important (as in the South) for access to the resources distributed by the organs of the state, especially since the Second World War. In close relation to these attitudes towards the centre, a tendency to segregation according to status and a strong concern with prestige among the elites and upper strata developed both in Spain and Italy. These status-concerned forces considered themselves to be the bearers of some of the most important attributes of the social order. They were guided by narrow status premises and tended to segregate themselves even from similar occupational groups originating in other regions. These narrowly oriented forces tended to conceive their legitimation to act in the political sphere in terms of their embodying prestigious symbols related to central aspects of the social order. This trend was particularly pronounced in Spain.[15] In Italy, the local elites only temporarily succeeded in basing their hold on the state on their traditional attributes. They soon lost positions to activists of the workers' parties and union leaders.[16]

In addition, the Southern European elites have conceived their role as one of mediation in the socio-political sphere; singular to such orientations has been the fact that the elites seldom performed these mediation tasks with a sense of commitment to the centre. Rather, their mediation seems to have been related to partisan interests. Consequently they have lacked legitimation and suffered from a refusal by broader social groups to see in them the most suitable proponents, of popular interests, even if there was some agreement that the mediators should represent the common good and be allied to the social forces they represented.

In practice, however, relations with the broader strata have been conducted primarily by forceful means or through particularistic networks of clientelism. Accordingly, the centres and their elites have been oriented by exclusive policies against forces they considered threatening to existing political formulas, or by attempts to incorporate these social and political forces on the basis of their passively accepting the existing rules of the political game. A related trend which developed in Southern European politics was a strong tendency towards a mushrooming of different political forces. That is, social forces tended to become politically fragmented around narrowly defined demands and issues. The elites of these countries were extremely fragmented and their internal differences were often considered irreconcilable; only during the periods of strong anarchy, colonial expansionism, or high concentration of power (like in Franco's regime), was dissent temporarily diminished, or at least ceased to undermine the political and administrative organs.[17] It seems that the Italian political forces were more prone to avoid dissent during periods of struggle than the Spanish;

thus, the different components of Italian *resistenza* managed to collaborate in order to attain common aims, while the Spanish forces opposing Franco remained divided along partisan lines even during the Civil War.

This fragility of alliances flourished even under conditions of open contest, such as those in Spain during the first half of the 19th century, or in Italy during the second postwar electoral regime, when political forces promoted parliamentary and constitutional crises in order to maximize short term gains,[18] which, in turn reinforced the fragility of the commitment to the state among the broader strata.

Conclusion

A detailed analysis of historical developments, of trends of centre formation and restructuring following political changes and/or the incorporation or rejection of demands and protest, is beyond the scope of this chapter. I hope, nevertheless, that preliminary indications were provided concerning traits of specificity in the moulding of the political realm in the countries under consideration, especially in connection with the interrelation of structural factors and the cultural perceptions of a proper structuring of the socio-political order, as carried and remodelled by the forces participating in shaping its contours. Basically, Southern European politics seem to have been characterized by the elites' orientations to the political centre, along with essentially fragile alliances, mushrooming of political forces, and drives on the latter's part to impose mediation in terms unlikely to gain full cultural legitimation. In addition, this study has indicated some of the fundamental conditions which brought about the centres perceiving social and regional plurality as a factor endangering collective identity, and, as a result, the propensity of central political elites, particularly in Spain, towards centralisation and suppression of peculiarities. It also shows the tendency of struggles to become oriented towards the political realm and to be articulated against symbols and structures of the political centre. Concrete political arrangements were perceived to be merely the result of a relation of forces, devoid of long-range legitimacy, and therefore became a focus for continuous struggle and were granted a low degree of mutual commitment. Accordingly, while various movements of protest were effective to varying degrees on issues regarding the specific structuring of distributive justice in the social system, they also elicited responses which did not enhance the political system's flexibility in dealing with issues such as specifying the contours of the collective identity, and the broader terms of political legitimacy. As soon as protest became involved in such issues, it was not handled in such a way which furthered its incorporation into the routine workings of the political system. Rather, the experience of the most 'successful' movements of protest and opposition—such as the fascists and the Franquist forces—highlights the fact that success (albeit momentary and vulnerable) in such an endeavour, in this cultural area, was mostly related to a totalistic, highly comprehensive and centralised vision of society.

Notes

1. In these societies themselves, discussions were going on about the nature of their political specificites. Italy is a case in point; there, both scholars and public servants and politicians discussed widely and for years the 'Southern issue'. See B. Caizzi, (ed.) *Nuova antologia della questione meridionale*, Milano, Edizioni di Comunitá, 1973.

2. See for instance N. Diamandouros, *Southern Europe. An Introductory Bibliographical Essay*, University of Strathclyde Studies in Public Policy, 1980; and G. Pridham, 'Comparative Perspectives on the New Mediterranean Democracies: A Model of Regime Transition?', *West European Politics*, 7, 1984, pp. 1–29.

3. C. Levi-Strauss, *Structural Anthropology*, New York, Basic Books, 1963.

4. Bibliographical references are omitted here. Comprehensive historical analyses are provided by R. Carr, *España, 1808–1939*, Barcelona, Ariel, 1978; and M. Clark, *Modern Italy, 1871–1982*, London and New York, Longman, 1984. Further references see in H. Driessen and D. Meertens, *A Selected Bibliography on Spanish Society*, University of Amsterdam Papers on European and Mediterranean Societies, 1976.

5. When the King tried to effect changes in the established rules of political life, as did Amedeo of Savoja in the 1870s, the principal political actors perceived this action as partisan and openly opposed it. Similarly, during the so-called 'monarchic' (without a King) period of Franquist rule, the concentration of power in the executive notwithstanding, Franco retained the style of ideal rulership; he seldom interrupted cabinet discussions, and remained aloof and imperturbable during the quarrels of his ministers, who represented a disparate spectrum of social forces supporting the regime of the *Caudillo*. With the assumption of power by Juan Carlos I upon Franco's death in 1975, the new King likewise opted to take little part in the daily affairs of state, even though he retained control of nominations to positions of effective state direction, and remained the ultimate source of legitimacy and authority. This characteristic was evident in the course of the failed efforts of Tejero and his allies to take power (through *pronunciamientos*) in the early 1980s. See Carr, *España*, pp. 310–18; C. Alba, 'On

Spain after Franco', unpublished manuscript, 1979; and J. Maravall, *The Transition to Democracy in Spain*, London, Croom Helm, 1982, respectively.

6. On Spain see for instance the titles of the excellent series *Historia de los movimientos sociales* published by Siglo XXI. E. G. J. A. Duran, *Agrarismo y movilización campesina en el país gallego (1875–1912)*, Madrid, 1977.

7. In Italy this characteristic was typical only of the period that preceded Italian unification and of the fascist period.

8. System supportiveness has become more widespread among Spanish party leaders and other elite sectors under conditions of open political contest during the transition to democracy of the late 1970s and 1980s. Observers relate this change to the critical experience of the Civil War; similarly, the fact that the transition accommodated entrenched social forces and interests of the previous regime, facilitated the mutual recognition of the 'old' and 'new' leaderships. 'Perhaps the secret of Spain's success . . . is the very fact that the transition to democracy was initiated and lead throughout by the legitimate heirs of the dictator. This, plus the fact that this leadership made it a point of skilfully using the constitutional means offered by the dictatorship itself to achieve the explicit aim of full electoral competition, forestalled, coopted, and even transformed two likely sources of dissent: dissent from the unrepented nostalgies of the dictator, and dissent from those opponents of the same who were entitled to suspect a transition guided of all (*sic*) by *los de siempre*.' G. Di Palma, 'Government Performance: An Issue and Three Cases in Search of Theory', p. 181 in *West European Politics*, 7, 1984, pp. 172–187.

9. See R. Aya, *The Missed Revolution*, University of Amsterdam Papers on European and Mediterranean Societies, 1975.

10. On the Catalonian case for instance see *Catalunya soto el regim franquista*, Paris, 1973; J. Rossinyol, *Le probleme national catalan*, Paris, 1974; E. C. Hansen, *Rural Catalonia under the Franco Regime*, Cambridge, Cambridge University Press, 1977; and W. T. Salisbury and J. D. Theberge, (eds.) *Spain in the 1970s*, New York, Praeger, 1976.

11. In the initial period, the central political forces allowed the Southern *notabili* to rule the *Mezzogiorno* until the rise of fascism; the low representativity of these elites was conducive to a certain amount of coalescing of social protest with separatist demands, which were also fostered by the Church and the old Borbonic elites that opposed the centre. The colonial expansion of Italy, the rise of fascism and indirectly, the migration of wide segments of the population, weakened the regionalist movements in the South. During Mussolini's rule, the centre tried to establish direct rule in the South. Since the 1960s, administrative autonomy has been granted to frontier regions in the North and to the Islands of Sicily and Sardinia, and a distributive policy was implemented through the Cassa per il Mezzogiorno, while political separatism seemed to be declining. On some of these aspects see S. N. Eisenstadt and L. Roniger, *Patrons, Clients and Friends*, Cam-

bridge University Press, 1984, pp. 64–71 and bibliographical references there.

12. It should be emphasized that, paradoxically enough, such situations arose in Italy partly despite and partly due to secular–religious polarisation, a relatively late process of secularisation of legitimacy, and the relative organisational weakness of the political centre formed in the late nineteenth century.

13. See J. H. Merryman, *The Civil Law Tradition*, Stanford, Stanford University Press, 1969; J. H. Merryman and D. S. Clark, (eds.) *Comparative Law*, Indianapolis, Bobbs-Merrill, 1978; and J. Finnis, *Natural Law and Natural Rights*, Oxford, Clarendon Press, 1980.

14. Pragmatism in Italy probably was related to the communal urban traditions that crystallised in the fifteenth and sixteenth centuries, and to the entrepreneurial orientations that subsequently flourished in Northern Italy and, to a certain extent, in Central Italy as well. Needless to say, pragmatism has not been a sufficient condition for assuring alliances during political crises such as that of the early 1920s. During that period, the failure of the major Catholic and Socialist parties to confer high priority to the safeguard of individual and collective Liberal freedoms hindered their ability to join forces in opposition to the fascists.

15. For example, the Grant Corps in Spain, which provided 57 per cent of all general directors of Spanish ministries from 1938 to 1974. See my article on 'Social Stratification in Southern Europe' in Chapter 7 of this book.

16. This process probably contributed to the devaluation of the prestige of political activity as an occupation from the late 1900s to the end of the Second World War.

17. It is too early to judge whether the period of transition to democracy from the late 1970s onwards has engendered new and lasting patterns of political participation.

18. See for instance A. Zuckerman, *Political Clienteles in Power*, London and Beverly Hills, Sage, 1975.

4 Some programmatic notes towards a comparative study of student protest: the English and Italian cases

*Sara Levinthal**

The problem

Protest by students is not new in the history of human society. Violent student protest was already existent in the Middle Ages, while protest and political activism by students, especially as parts of wider social and national movements, have been an integral part of the history of modern society. Similarly, various types of adolescent rebellions rooted to no small degree, in generational discontinuity or conflict, can, as is well known, be found throughout the history of human society.[1] But beyond these features student protests in the 1960s evinced also some new ones. The student protest which developed in Western Europe and North America during the 1960s was more comprehensively hostile to authority than was any previous student movement.[2] It tended to be hostile to authority on principle, whereas its predecessors had tended to be hostile to particular authorities. Furthermore, during the 1960s protest erupted around issues with little relation to those which were at the heart of student protest in the past: the demand for 'student power', their demand for an end to 'in locum parentis' authority of the universities over the students. Moreover, many of these movements tended to combine their political activity with violence and destructive orientations which often went far beyond the earlier Bohemian traditions of youth or artistic intellectual subcultures. These movements expressed a very far-reaching, general and widespread alienation from the existing social order. Furthermore, unlike earlier student protest which tended to be restricted to a small part of the student body, in the sixties such protest elicited either the support, or at least the sympathy, of a large proportion of the student population.

In general student protest in the 1960s has been explained by a shift of the foci of protest in modern society from demands to participate in

*Thanks are due to Jon Simons for his help in preparing these Notes.

the centres to a focus on the search for new *loci* of meaningful participation beyond the existing socio-political centres on one hand and the convergence and mutual reinforcement of intellectual antinomianism, and generational discontinuity and conflict, on the other. However, despite these general similarities, there were important differences in the characteristics of student protest in the 1960s in different countries. In the following we intend to point out the specific characteristics of student protest in England and Italy during this period, with particular reference to the tendency of student protest in England to be less intense, less widespread and more institutionalised than student protest in other Western European nations during this period.

The divergent development of student protest in England and Italy

Italy[3]

Student unrest began as the national union of students, 'UNURI', proved ineffective in lobbying for reform. The socialist UGI and Catholic INTESA groups within the UNURI pressed for an unsuccessful occupation at Rome in 1960. The initiative developed a local focus, leaders emerged and faded rapidly, as occupations took place in Milan, Rome, Naples, Florence, Venice, Trent and Pisa.

The most common activity was the occupation of the University, disrupting all teaching and often introducing rather chaotic (alternative) seminars and group debates. Alongside the attempt to construct an alternative curriculum, students also took to the streets and by 1968 riots provoked bitter police reaction, as in Rome. In the wake of this reaction, protest began to change its form and by 1969 leftist student groups diverted their energies to agitation in factories and farms. Workers struck and occupied industrial plants winning for themselves (with student help) gains in the negotiation of national labour contracts. Some student groups such as the *Lotta Continua*, continued the spirit of student revolt by relying on constant activism and local autonomy. Others namely the UCIMI, a rigid Stalinist group, combined a 'democratic centralist' organisational framework with charismatic leadership. In the seventies, student protest as such faded away.

Moving specifically to student goals and ideas, the trend seems to have been for protest to become increasingly radical and to acquire an ever widening scope. Thus, in the early sixties, students tried to influence programmes and curricula. At Trent, for instance, students wanted the Institute of Social Sciences and the National Government to recognise studies for a degree in sociology; having achieved this in 1965 they pressed for changes in the courses to develop a more critical approach to society. In a parallel manner students in Italy demanded the recognition of their participation in the running of universities and when this was rejected they moved to take control of the university. At Turin, the idea of permanent struggle against academic authority was generated and came to embrace all forms of authority; protest ceased to be a means and gradually became an end in itself. Students in the UGI considered that education could not be reformed under neo-capitalism, a view shared by 65 per cent of Roman students in 1969.

In Milan students of architecture questioned the type of social reform they were expected to achieve through their impact on the environment. Trent students insisted on the need for a critical awareness of society, using a mixture of Marxism and the ideas of the German student leader, Rudi Dutschke. They saw the university as a factory producing skilled graduates as a commodity for the market. At Turin, Marcuse and Fromm inspired student attacks on figures of authority. Students argued that university teaching was designed to produce submissive characters. This anti-authoritarianism was the theme of the movement nationally. With time, 'the enemy' was perceived as the system which followed the dictates of a bureaucratic, 'functional' rationality. Students felt they were expected to play the role of social manipulators, using their knowledge to run a 'machine society' which required social engineers; hence the need for social scientists, architects, and producers of mass culture. Students thus rebelled against their contradictory position in society: where they were manipulated at university in order to manipulate others later, but would never be allowed to criticise the overall irrationality of the system. For the students the only alternative to the existing regimented, bureaucratic society was an open, participatory community based on direct human relationships and spontaneity.

In addition to those seeking to build a 'Utopian' communality were those Maoist, Leninist and Trotskyist groups that stressed the organisation of the workers and believed in violent systemic revolution. As a result these groups oriented their activities towards a coalition of students and workers, to detach workers from their loyalty to reformist trade unions and the PCI.

England[4]

During the 1960s, student activism in England developed in a bell-shaped pattern starting as a localised campus debate, expanding into wider protest supported by a large percentage of the student body, and finally fading as the leadership lost support of students and factional rivalry grew. This protest movement developed within the established frameworks of English student politics.

Student unrest began at the London School of Economics (LSE) in 1966, and tension between students and the School's authorities provoked an occupation in March 1967. In the meantime, the Radical Students Alliance was formed as a challenge to the more conventional National Students Union. There were a few short sit-ins in 1967, and in 1968 there were demonstrations against speakers visiting campuses, at Sussex, Essex, Manchester, Cambridge and elsewhere. Occupations took place in 1968 at Hornsey and Guildford art colleges, and sit-ins in Manchester. The last significant event was another brief occupation at the LSE after the school had been closed for three weeks.

The protest itself tended to focus on the issues of the Vietnam War and racism. In particular, how these issues were expressed on campus, in such events as the university authorities welcoming speakers who supported the Vietnam War or the raising of fees for foreign students. Students felt that protest to such events expressed what they assumed to be commonly held moral and ethical premises, such as principles of human rights, social tolerance and racial equality. Anti-authoritarian positions were rare and tended to be restricted to art students. There was also a second level of protest issues. These tended to be concerned with what students considered to be 'their right' to influence school policies. These issues focused on students' demands to be represented in the schools' administration, to have unrestricted use of school buildings and to end what they perceived to be the 'victimisation' of student leaders by the administration. These issues implied a change in the relations of power on the campuses. The most extreme case was the demand by art students to be allowed to 'entirely reconstruct the system of art education'.

However, as the movement gained strength on campus, factional rivalry developed within the leadership. Thus, as student protest began to spread to wider issues, such as student power on campus and national government policies, sectarian struggles increased within the leadership. During this stage, the tactics of some of the students became more violent and the universities' administrations began to turn to the police more often to restore order on the campuses. Opinions among the students at large became increasingly polarised. More and more students objected to the violent tactics of some of the student activists. As a result, the more radical elements became increasingly marginal within the protest movement. The leadership divided into sectarian factions and the movement began to wane. The majority of the activisits realigned themselves with the major political parties or returned to academic activities, a minority joining far-left splinter groups. On the whole, however, English student protest was less militant, more orderly, less violent and more integrated into the established channels of student politics than were its continental counterparts.

Great Britain had the lowest reported student political activism and the lowest reported degree of support for student protest in Europe; it was the least militant, the least anti-authoritarian, and the most integrated into the established frameworks of student unionism. Thus, compared to Italy, student actions in England were brief and localised and more centered on aspects on student life *per se*. Moreover, whereas in Italy student activity was focused on bringing about an alternative model of social order, in England it generally remained focused on academic issues. Even when students raised broader issues, such as racism, colonialism, or opposition to the Labour Government, they did not do so as part of an attempt to recreate or restructure the social order *tout court*.

A possible framework of interpretation of student protest

As can be seen, despite certain similarities, the path, characteristics and social impact of student protest in both Britain and Italy were strikingly dissimilar. A divergence which can perhaps be best summed up in the contrast between the totalistic, Utopian cast of Italian protest as opposed to the more short-term, relatively circumscribed and student-specific nature of the goals of their English counterparts can be seen.

In the past most attempts to account for these differences have remained bound to analyses of the institutional structures of the English and Italian universities, the respective marketability of the skills students acquired and differences in their respective social backgrounds. A number of scholars have however sought to go beyond existing explanations, especially in the context of English development. Thus the debate between Perry Anderson, Tom Nairn and E. P. Thompson on the 'peculiarities of the English' included recognition that England's failure to experience student rebellion on a 'continental scale' was somehow connected to the specificities of its historical development.[5]

This insight, as tantalising as it is in its implications has yet to be subjected to more far-reaching sociological research. In the following we shall attempt to provide some rudimentary indications on the possible connection between student protest in the mid-twentieth century and more long-term patterns and developments in Italy and England. Specifically by taking account of the respective structuring of the English and Italian centres and the nature of participation of elite groups and intellectuals within the polity we believe a greater appreciation of the specificities of protest in each case may be achieved.

The Italian background[6]

Many of the characteristics of student protests during the 1960s resembled the traditional modes of participation of Italian intellectuals in earlier protest movements. Three major patterns of relationships of intellectuals to the polity existed in Italy. One consisted of individual patronage and sponsorship of intellectuals by the economic and political ruling elites. A second was that of intellectuals who tried to influence the polity through institutional structures, as typical of the Catholic intelligentsia. A third pattern involved intellectuals with independent means, active politically, writing and debating ideas of the social order that would have been unacceptable to the social forces in power. The latter were particularly active in Italian politics since the *Risorgimento*.

It was from among this last category that most intellectuals involved in protest movements in Italy were recruited. At least since the *Risorgimento*, most of these tended to advocate highly ideological, often intensely sectarian, positions and were usually organised into small protest groups, which attempted to reach out to broader (oppressed) social groups. These intellectuals tended to portray themselves as the only 'true leaders' of Italy. This self-perception contrasted sharply with their objective marginality within the protest movements in which they were active. In fact, in these movements intellectuals tended to become less influential than army officers, local nobility, or later, representatives of the trade unions, as soon as the movements began to attract wider popular support. When this happened most intellectuals were pushed back into the sidelines of Italian politics.

The rapid growth of higher education in Italy following World War II moderated the marginality of Italian intellectuals within the polity by expanding the need for professionally trained personnel who found employment within the expanding institutional structures of the centre. One of the by-products of these changes was that the number of university students in Italy rose rapidly. However, these changes were not matched by reforms of either the universities or the educational system. This provided an issue of grievance among Italian students and was one of the initial demands of student protest during the early 1960s.

The expansion of the occupational market came to an end in the mid-1960s just as there was another increase in the number of university students. This increase was even more rapid than that following World War II. A growth in the number of students attending universities in Italy though was not matched by the number of those graduating nor by the opportunities available to them, which led to growing unemployment among university graduates and a tendency for students to study for longer periods of time 'parked' at the universities. This resulted in a growing number of dissatisfied students who took part in the 1960s 'student revolt'.

A number of similarities can be discerned between the roles of Italian intellectuals in protest and politics in earlier periods of Italian history and those of student protesters during the 1960s. During the 1960s 'student revolt' students tended to form small, highly ideological and often intensely sectarian organisations, each of which felt that it was the leader of the vanguard of the 'coming revolution'. Most of the students involved in these protests had some independent economic means and were not dependent upon the institutional structures of the centre for employment. The small groups of student protesters tried to lead workers in labour disputes. Finally, by the late 1960s the majority of Italian students returned to their studies, while some of the protest organisations evolved into urban guerilla groups and others were absorbed 'in toto' into the political system. Such a pattern of activity brings to mind some characteristics of earlier groups of Italian elites in their impingement on the social centre. For instance, during the *Risorgimento* intellectuals 'went South' in an attempt to lead peasants in a revolt for an independent Italy. They were highly committed ideologically, yet divided into sectarian groups and as with the students they too either left off their protest activities to return to their professional practice, or developed new organisational frameworks, which continued a radical and violent confrontation with the centre. A small number of them were absorbed directly into the political system, usually holding secondary positions in it.

Student protest in Italy during the 1960s was structured by the basic characteristics of the Italian polity. Italian politics tended to be organised on two separate levels: one of intense ideological debate and another of pragmatic, concrete policies, reflecting the interests of the groups in power. Each major elite group and most of the major factions within those groups believed that they individually had the right to rule. This resulted in a strong tendency towards factional rivalry and a highly fragmented nature in Italian politics. Yet at the same time the political system was perceived as an arena to actualise particularistic interests; mediation and pragmatism were highly emphasised and unstable coalitions succeeded one another in searching for power and short-term gains.

Political practice took place within a centre, characterised by a deep division between sectarian and regional allegiances and by the perception of government as expressing the political hegemony of the party in power. Very few challenges to the legitimacy of the centre were made as larger sections of Italy's political groups accepted de facto, at least to some degree, their incorporation into the polity.

Student protest reflected the geographic dispersion characteristic of the Italian polity. It was centred in the Northern universities whereas in the South little unrest was in evidence. Student protest, in its highly sectarian, minimal degree of national coordination and low organisational strength, tended to reflect the sectarian and intensely ideological characteristics of political rhetoric in Italy. Similarly as earlier Italian political elites, students tended to sustain the claim that they were true leaders of the masses in the Italian polity. In addition the growing left-wing militancy that developed in the later period of student protest was a response to the contradictory nature of Italian politics. The Communist Party support of the Christian Democratic government, led militant student activists to radicalise positions as a proper answer to the 'betrayal' of the communists. Working in opposite directions but connected to Italian political pragmatism was the fact that the majority of Italian students did not accept the call of their leaders to boycott the national polity or to join 'with the workers' in direct confrontation with the State thus reflecting the widespread acceptance of the legitimacy of the centre by Italian student protesters. While political violence was directed against bankers, judges or police officials, the Parliament was not attacked.

In sum, the highly ideological and intensely sectarian tendencies of Italian student protest along with little national organisation or coordination, seems to have reflected the basic characteristics of both the modes of participation of intellectuals in earlier political protest movements and the contradictions between the ideological and pragmatic levels of Italian politics. In addition, many of these characteristics also reflected the deeply embedded nature of Italian intellectuals who tended to be highly ideological and to have very little pressures upon them to accept more pragmatic positions.

The English background

On the whole English students, unlike most other student protesters of the period, did not reject authority on principle, but opposed specific actions by specific authorities. They did not reject the existing political system, either its symbols or its institutions. This was unique among student protests of the period. There was also a tendency for the majority of England's student activists to re-orient themselves within the established political left, the Labour Party, when the radical factions within the general protest movement began to push strongly for what they considered overall opposition to the political system. During this process these more militant factions tended to become increasingly marginal within the protest movement in general and were apt to end up as highly sectarian left-wing splinter groups.

In fact, many of the specific characteristics of student protest in England during the 1960s strongly resembled those of English protest politics during earlier periods. In England the sovereignty of the centre had been accepted by most elite groups from very early in English history. Moreover, very early in its history a strong emphasis on collective identity developed. Mutual commitments among elite groups led to their growing autonomy. It should be pointed out that the need to establish stable coalitions among elite groups occurred in many parts of Europe but only in England did these groups share a common commitment to the centre itself. Protest movements that emerged in England acted within these confines, structuring what may be called the English mode of incorporation of protest. Throughout England's history there have been protest movements. These have usually been made up of a coalition of forces that have agreed to work together in order to try to achieve some specific goal. At the same time, they have however, tended to reaffirm the legitimacy of the existing institutions of the polity.

In consequence, whenever a faction within a protest movement moved to deny the right of the whole of the public body to decide collectively the nature of power, then the faction in question tended to become increasingly marginalised. Political factions that denied the authority of the centre as well as the rights of the principal political participants to be part of that framework tended to become increasingly peripheral within English protest movements (as those movements became increasingly integrated into the polity). At that point the coalition of forces that made up the protest movement began to disintegrate, the majority realigning themselves with the centre and often with the ruling coalition while the minority moved into the political sidelines. This was precisely the dynamic which characterised English student protest in the 1960s.

However, student protest in the 1960s in England was not only influenced by the major general characteristics of protest and politics in England. It was also modelled along the traditional lines of participation in the polity. In England as in many parts of Europe, intellectuals were usually recruited from social circles that were subordinate to the ruling elites. However, in England, unlike in other parts of Europe, from at least the period of the Reformation, these social groups had some degree of direct access to the institutions of government, particularly to Parliament. Moreover, although class boundaries in England were distinct, there was throughout English history a certain degree of sponsored mobility into the upper classes. Education was one of the most important of these channels. Intellectuals could, and many did, assume the life styles of elite groups with which they were associated. However, despite the interwoven relationship of most intellectuals, with England's ruling elites, intellectuals retained an autonomous sphere of activities. This was due to the fact that, despite their associations with various social elites and despite the fact that they did not form an identifiable social strata, most intellectuals acted as articulators of political ideals within whichever group they were associated with. This led, to their identification as 'brokers of ideas' within protest movements and at least to some extent within the polity at large. In addition, unlike other parts of Europe, the audience listening to these debates tended to be very wide. This meant that the degree of influence intellectuals in England had was much greater than that of intellectuals in other parts of Europe.

As can be seen certain characteristics of student protest during the 1960s were similar to the major characteristics of the English polity and to the nature of the relationships of English intellectuals to politics and protest. Students in fact demanded to be considered intellectuals, their claims often revolved around their 'rights' to articulate and influence the 'moral standing' of society, or at least of their 'schools'. Students interpreted their demands to end racism and expand the scope of social welfare as part of their responsibility *as intellectuals* to guide English society and to advocate 'true' social justice.

Indeed, in this claim they seem to have been following the lead opened by the Campaign for Nuclear Disarmament (CND), which gave a new legitimacy and provided novel models for the role–expectations of intellectuals within the polity. CND had widespread support among the intellectual and professional community and can be described as a left-wing intellectual movement. It was not the first left-wing intellectual protest movement in England—the 'King and Country' debates during the 1930s cannot be forgotten. The CND, however, was the first protest movement of intellectuals during the twentieth century that took to the streets to demonstrate political demands. This combination of political debate and street demonstrations influenced the issues and forms that students protest took during the 1960s.

Taking these factors into consideration, we can begin to understand why student protest in England during the 1960s tended to start by focusing on the 'arbitrary' nature of university authority and not authority in general. For the content of the most common demands of English student protests during the 1960s expressed what most students thought the roles of intellectuals should be. These orientations were reinforced by both the general English orientation that emphasised popular consent, as the basis of authority and orientations concerning the need for 'the people' to control the forces that shape their lives. The bell-shaped development of the waves of student protest, the rise at the beginning, swelling into widespread support followed by increased marginalisation of radical groups within the protest movement as the majority of students begin to withdraw their support from the violent tactics of 'direct action' is at least similar to the pattern of marginalisation of radical factions within earlier protest movements. Even the decision by left activists, marginalised within the protest movements to 'permeate', as the Fabians had called it, the Labour Party was at least similar to the patterns of incorporation of protest established earlier in England.

Concluding perspectives

As is the case with protest movements in general, student protest developed a tendency to focus demands on the right to participate in society's central orders. Students tended as well to legitimise their claims in terms of the social and political traditions of their societies. In England this tradition emphasised the right of different social groups, especially elite groups of various natures, to have access to the centre which was moreover perceived as a focus of national identity. The centre and its institutions were perceived as sovereign and independent. As a consequence the demands of protest movements to participate in this centre entailed an acceptance of the institutions and symbols of the centre. The level of protest and the range of issues around which protest developed tended accordingly to be limited and usually focused on social reform and not an overall structural change. There were extremist elements in every protest movement. However as the movement as a whole orientated its demands to the centre these elements were forced to the sidelines of protest movements. Concomitantly the issues raised during protest were absorbed and so enhanced the flexibility and legitimacy of the centre.

Student protest in England focused on demands for social or institutional reform at the level of national or university policy. The issues they focused on dealt primarily with ethical and moral issues related to the conduct of either the national or university collective. These demands, in essence, re-affirmed the students' basic acceptance of the legitimacy and sovereignty of the collective in question and its institutional structure. Similar to earlier cases of intellectual participation in the polity, the demands students raised in the 1960's tended to be phrased in social and ethical terms.

At the same time, similar to earlier protest movements among intellectuals, student protest in England during the 1960's tended to focus on symbolic debates within the pre-existing institutional structures of student politics. In fact, it was a protest movement almost exclusively made up of organisational activities. Declarations and democratic resolutions played an important part in student protest in England during this period. All of these characteristics reflect the students' basic acceptance of the legitimacy of those institutions within which they were acting. They perceived themselves as an identifiable elite, as intellectuals reaffirming what they perceived to be the place of intellectuals within the English polity. And as such, they were demanding what they perceived to be their 'right' to influence the centre's social and academic policies. Thus, in England, students did not tend to express extreme anti-authoritarian positions common in other parts of Europe.

By contrast, the Italian polity was characterised by the existence of strong centrifugal tendencies and a lack of widespread commitment in respect to the centre. In fact after a short period of activism which led to the establishment of a nation–state in the mid-nineteenth century, the State's legitimacy to represent the national collectivity and to be the true expression of the social order was contested by social forces and elites representing either particular interests or by those who accepted the primacy of the Church. While in practice these forces were gradually incorporated into the centre and came to accept it on a pragmatic level, conflicts over the basic parameters of the socio-cultural order continued to characterise political action in Italy. As a result, even locally orientated, circumscribed protest took on the attributes of a major challenge to the social order and to the centre. Similarly the response of the centre to these demands did not necessarily enhance its legitimacy or organisational flexibility. As we have seen student protest in Italy soon developed an orientation to the total restructuring of society, positing an alternative model of the social order. This was expressed in intensely political terms and was characterised by an extremist symbolic rhetoric similar to that of Italian political and intellectual elites existing beyond the parameters of the centre.

The preceding suggests that the forms taken by student protest in Italy and England during the 1960's were modelled according to the traditions of the polity and the forms of participation which elites in general and intellectuals in particular developed in both societies. These indications suggest that there is a need for further research into the comparative study of student protest. A more detailed research agenda would, we believe, take into account both the concrete development of student protest emphasised in existing literature as well as the structure of the centres and the forms of elite impingement along the programmatic lines indicated above.

Notes

1. On generational discontinuity and conflict see S. N. Eisenstadt, *From Generation to Generation*, Glencoe, Ill., Free Press, 1956.

2. L. Ferner, *The Conflict of Generations*, New York, Basic Books, 1969; also E. Shils, 'Tradition and Liberty, Autonomy and Interdependence', *Ethics* 68 1958, pp. 153–65.

3. On student protest in Italy see G. Statera, *Death of a Utopia: The Development and Decline of Student Movements in Europe*, New York, Oxford University Press, 1975; G. Artinotti, 'Positive Marginality: Notes on Italian Students in Periods of Political Mobilization', pp. 167–201 in S. M. Lipset and P. Altbach, (eds.), *Students in Revolt*, Boston, Beacon Press, 1970; and A. Mineo, 'The Italian Student Movement', pp. 115–21 in J. Nagel, (ed.), *Student Power*, London, Merlin Press, 1969.

4. On England, see A. Cockburn and R. Blackburn, (eds), *Student Power*, Harmondworth, Penguin, 1970; A. Habey and S. Marks, 'British Student Politics', pp. 35–59 in S. M. Lipset and R. Atlbach, *Students in Revolt*, Boston, Beacon Press, 1970; and M. S. Archer, *Students, University, and Society*, London, Heinemann, 1972.

5. P. Anderson, 'Components of the National Culture', pp. 214–84 in Cock-

burn and Blackburn, *Student Power*; E. P. Thompson, 'The Peculiarity of the English', pp. 35–91 in idem, *The Poverty of Theory*, London, Merlin Press, 1975; P. Anderson, 'Origin of the Present Crisis', *New Left Review*, **23** 1964 pp. 24–53; T. Nairn, 'The English Working class', pp. 187–206 in, R. Blackburn, *Ideology in the Social Sciences*, Fontana, 1972; and E. Hobsbawn, 'Intellectuals in the Labour Movement', *Marxism Today*, July 1979, pp. 212–20.

6. References to the historical background drawn upon for the following analysis have been omitted. For the analytical perspective followed and the characteristics of these European social formations see S. N. Eisenstadt, *Revolution and the Transformation of Societies*, New York, Free Press, 1978. On the place of intellectuals in society see S. N. Eisenstadt and S. R. Graubard, eds., *Intellectuals and Tradition*, New York, Humanities Press, 1973, especially T. F. O'Dea, 'The role of the Intellectual in the Catholic Tradition', pp. 150–89; and G. B. de Hussar, (ed.), *The Intellectuals: A Controversial Portrait*, New York, Free Press, 1960.

5 The failure of socialism in the United States: a reconsideration

Adam Seligman

Introduction

The object of the following study is to offer some new perspectives on one of the most blatant lacunae in American socio-political life: the absence of an organisationally strong, ideologically coherent and politically autonomous socialist movement and party in the United States. In contrast to North America, most socialist parties which emerged in the industrialised societies of Western Europe have played an important role, both politically and culturally, in structuring collective life. The failure of similar developments in the United States has been the subject of different analyses. We will here briefly review these analyses, examine some of their problematic aspects and present an alternative perspective.

Socialism as a formally organised movement in the United States has been, save during one decade or so, a rather weak and electorally insignificant political force; its role in shaping collective life and orientations has also been minimal. This anomaly has been the focus of a debate initiated by Werner Sombart's question in his famous essay, 'Why There Is No Socialism in the United States?'.[1] The incongruity between American social developments and the 'classic' hypothesis of the development of socialism has been the *bête noire* of Marxists, socialists and other social analysts even prior to Sombart's seminal work. A number of basic features, both of American capitalist development and of the socialist movement itself, will serve to elucidate this incongruity.

The economy and society of the United States have been characterized by a high rate of urbanisation, fully-developed and expanding industry, strong well-organised labour unions with wide bases of support and power and by a system of democratic politics which have facilitated the potential organisation of different interests and demands. The socialism that developed within this context, however, lacked the ideological and organisational salience to be expected in such circumstances. The ideology of socialism in the United States, in contrast to its European counterparts was distinctly non-radical; its goals were very similar to those of the American political system proper; the movement was not class-based and suffered extensively from internal schisms (both towards the centre and the left). Thus, socialism in the United States was radically different in structural meaning to the movement in Europe.

Defining characteristics of the socialist movement in the United States

From the many historical and sociological studies of socialism in the United States, one may abstract a number of defining characteristics which present the central problems for an analysis of American socialism.[2] They can be summarised as follows:

Ideology: American socialist ideology was heterodox in its socio-political orientations; it contained strains of anarchism, syndicalism, Marxism and a strong Christian moral ethos. These heterodox orientations rooted in different visions of man, society and the nature of the interrelations between them, militated against the crystallisation of a coherent ideological position not only among the different socialist organisations, but within the Socialist Party itself.

Organisation: The movement was organisationally diversified and, up to 1919, the three main groups carrying socialist orientations were in continual conflict and rivalry. The emergence of the Communist Party after 1919, presented a further obstacle to unity or accommodation between the different organisational frameworks.

Social Base: Socialist organisations were alienated from the major strata and occupational groups which elsewhere had provided the main support for socialist programmes and platforms, namely the industrial working class.

The American Political System: The system had a unique capacity to reorient itself towards socialist demands, and to incorporate them as reform programmes and social desiderata. Twice, during Wilson's and Roosevelt's administrations, the Democratic Party incorporated many socialist demands and institutionalised them within the system. These examples 'hint' at a much broader characteristic of the American system: its plurality, flexibility and mobility to co-opt and absorb protest.

Economy: America's material wealth, and its system of distributive justice furthered social mobility and militated against the development of class-bound political consciousness, thereby limiting socialist development.

Social Heterogeneity and Ideological Diversity of Groups Supporting Socialism in the United States: The different social groups comprising the socialist movement—urban labour, immigrant groups, western labourers (lumberjacks, miners), farmers, southern Church groups, intellectuals—were divided organisationally among different frameworks, and articulated widely differing political orientations, ranging between European Marxism, industrial unionism, Christian Socialism and revolutionary unionism.

Nature of Internal Socialist Coalitions: For a movement to enter the basic coalition which constituted the Socialist Party, it had only to accept a minimal, rather loose platform calling for an end to the inequalities of capitalism. The result was that the criterion for membership was support of, and participation in the party, rather than a coherent socialist orientation; leading in turn, to de-emphasis of ideological goals and orientations. Moreover, Socialist elites did not enter broad coalitions with the major political forces in America. The AFL's brief period of tolerating the Socialist Party and its occasional willingness to work with socialist unions (such as the International Ladies Garment Workers Union and the Brewery Workers Union), are exceptions to the rule. Failure on the labour front was repeated in the political sphere. The socialists did not fulfill one of the most important prerequisites needed to penetrate the American political system—a broad coalition of interests.

Marginality of Socialist Elites: Socialist elites tended to remain on the periphery of American life. The support engendered by such figures as E. V. Debbs and Norman Thomas, for example, was a result of their moral tone as 'prophets', rather than their socialist policies or ideology.

The Nature of Socialist Demands: Whereas European socialism, which was rooted firmly in Marxist doctrine, stressed the class articulation of revolutionary symbolism, American socialism, with its strong moral element, emphasized the gradual rise towards a classless society. It eschewed violence and was committed to working within the system, as expressed in the nature of its demands and its themes of protest.

In concrete terms, socialist demands tended to focus on two specific issues: the demand for widening the areas of government intervention and activity in society, calling for more social services, schools and the provision of basic needs; and the demand for the collectivisation of industry, for which in contrast to Europe, concrete proposals were never made. In general, American socialism was reformist in nature, accepting much of the system and seeking more to remedy than to overthrow the basic patterns of collective life.

Analytic perspectives on the study of American socialism

A number of factors have been attributed to the continued failure of socialism in the United States. Those on the structural level may be summarised as follows:

(1) The high level of organisational diversity (the Socialist Party, Socialist Labour Party, Industrial Workers of the World (I.W.W.), later the Communist Party, the Communist Labour Party and the Workers' Party);
(2) The tactics of dual unionism advanced by both the I.W.W. and Socialist Labour Party later to be attempted by the Communists, which resulted in the hostility of organised labour and the AFL;
(3) A general alienation from the mainstream of the labour movement and its organisational structure;
(4) The ethnic nature of most socialist groups, which tended to lose their socialist ideology as they integrated into American life;
(5) The high degree of sectarianism and what D. Bell termed 'ideological rigidity' which characterised the movement as a whole and which, as Bell has argued, hampered the party in translating its revolutionary ideology into meaningful political action.[3]

These factors have in turn been increasingly related to a second set, which bears upon the wider structural aspects of American society and their role in limiting the development of socialism. The most prominent of these factors are: the absence of a feudal heritage, the open frontier, the general high degree of social mobility, the immigrant nature of American society, the nature of the political system and, of course, America's material wealth.

Absence of a feudal heritage

The absence of a feudal heritage prevented the emergence of a 'politics of class', and blurred the dividing line between the aristocracy (both landed and commercial) and the middle and especially lower classes, which in Europe contributed to the crystallisation of a class state and politics.[4] Moreover, the American lower classes, as opposed to the European, did not have to undergo a process of self-definition and crystallisation in order to secure certain basic social and civil rights (such as the franchise).[5] The lack of a feudal background was instrumental also in the formation of a social centre which focused on equality and the potential for equality, while those of modern Europe remained anchored in inequality and hierarchic notions of social structure. Finally, the absence of an indigenous aristocracy and the presence of a large, strong and independent middle stratum contributed to what has been termed the 'American middle class ethos'.[6] In other words, the economic and structural saliency of the entrepreneurial class was complemented by the ideology of the entrepreneur as 'cultural hero'.

Open frontier

The effect of the open frontier on the American socio-political system was a focal point in Sombart's analysis.[7] He stressed its role as a 'safety valve' through which radical and discontented elements in society could filter to the West, where they could establish a new society, or at least new institutional arrangements. Furthermore, Sombart recognised that beyond the actual opportunity the frontier offered, the cultural perception or consciousness of mobility implied by the frontier was an important factor in itself, differentiating the American from the European worker.

Social mobility

American society was characterised by structural openness and social mobility. Research on the relation of mobility to political attitudes was initiated by Sombart, and more recently conducted by, among others, Seymour Lipset, Reinhard Bendix and Stephen Thernstrom. Thernstrom noted that, 'High rates of occupational and property mobility and selective patterns of urban migration which weeded out the unsuccessful and constantly reshuffled them together produced a social context in which a united 'isolated mass' of dispossessed, disaffected workmen could not develop'.[8]

As in the case of the open frontier, beyond the actual possibilities for upward social mobility, the very consciousness and 'perception' of mobility was as important a factor in structuring American social and political attitudes: this belief in mobility tended '. . . to deflect potential radical protest into transvaluational religion or into hopes for children'.[9]

Status striving immigrants

The role played by immigrants was a factor in moulding American political attitudes. Immigrants sought acculturation in American society, accepting the status quo, and first generation Americans wanted to improve on their parents' inferior social status. This status striving served as reinforcement, influencing and informing predilections towards social conformity. The desire of many immigrants to 'achieve ascription' influenced their political orientations in a very definite manner—they tended to accept the major cultural models of American life in order to be accepted within the community.[10]

Political factors

A number of features of the American political system have been posited as relevant to the problem of socialism in America, the most important being the two-party system, and its ability to absorb and co-opt protest.

The two-party system, considered practically mandated by the constitution, makes third-party impingement virtually impossible. Moreover, it allows the major parties a high degree of flexibility to incorporate protest and co-opt 'manifest evidence of pervasive dissent', as can be seen for example in the phenomenon of socialist intellectuals and party members joining Roosevelt's administration, or the incorporation of abolitionists into the Republican Party and of populists into the Democratic Party.[11] Incorporation of certain platforms (such as increasing government intervention in various areas of social life during and after the Wilson era) led to a decrease in support for the socialists, who, while advocating the same reforms, couched them in terms of an overall restructuring of the socio-political system. Thus the system simultaneously incorporated 'bread-and-butter' issues, and delegitimised the accompanying ideology.

The comparative critique of past approaches and the emergence of a new line of inquiry

The search to define the parameters of American 'exceptionality' arose primarily out of an apparent insufficiency of those explanations of socialism's failure based solely on internal factors. Comparing developments in America with those in Europe and elsewhere has led to the conclusion that the uniqueness of the American experience lies neither solely in the major characteristics of its Socialist Party, nor in structural factors.

Socialist parties and movements throughout the world have always suffered splits and divergent ideological positions. The movement as a whole emerged from nineteenth century Utopian thought and even a perfunctory glance at French, Spanish, or Russian socialism, for example, immediately reveals the wide divergence in socio-political orientations and organisational frameworks. The point, then, is not that such ideological and organisational heterodoxy existed in the United States, but that a crystallisation or coalescence of ideological positions and organisational frameworks did not occur.

Similarly, a comparison with other societies lacking 'feudal baggage', such as Australia or Canada, where socialist parties with some political strength and saliency did develop, emphasises the need to go beyond existing perspectives as to the precise role of a 'feudal heritage' in structuring later forms of political practice, especially with regard to socialism.[12] A comparison of America with New Zealand or Australia also reveals the need to reassess the importance of the 'open frontier' in influencing the development of socialism, as in both these societies (which developed around, and in tension with, a frontier), radical politics and socialist parties did emerge.[13]

Reappraising the above factors has led to a growing realisation that the full scope of the pervasive ideological structure of the American social order, and its influence on the organisational and institutional aspects of social life must be taken into account. This has been evinced through research in a number of different yet interrelated areas. In his different analyses of socialist failure to penetrate the labour movement, for example, J. Laslett mentions the traditions and forms of American protest and its incorporation, as well as the importance of the prevailing ideological structure and its sociological and structural derivatives.[14] Such studies indicate the need for an analysis which combines structural components with an understanding of the role of 'Americanism' as an ideology in explaining the failure of socialism. Similarly, L. Hartz's analysis of the entrenchment of liberal–Lockean ideology in the ideology of 'Americanism', fails to explain the important content of this ideology—which proved crucial in anchoring political orientations in the major symbolic and institutional orders of the centre.[15]

An example of the interweaving of structural and symbolic dimensions can be found in Kurt Meyer's comparison of the American and Australian centres.[16] He points out the different institutional ambiances stemming from each centre's orientations: in Australia, the primary orientation was to the English centre—the 'fatherland' across the sea, which engendered tension between internal and external orientations towards centre construction. In America, however, such tension did not exist because from the start, the settlers defined their own symbolic realm of values and beliefs, independent of the socio-political centre in England. In fact, the early development of an autonomous or independent centre in colonial society, was one of the most important defining and differentiating characteristics of American society. Comparison with Canada, like Australia, reveals the need to expand the feudal heritage argument, too, along the lines of an analysis of ideology. For in Canada, as in the United States, *manhood sufferage* existed prior to the emergence of a mass working class movement; but in Canada, a viable socialist movement has existed, influencing parliamentary politics since the 1920's.[17] Thus, once again, the need to explain American uniqueness through other avenues is clearly apparent.

Furthermore, those studies focusing on the importance of upward social mobility and the 'embourgeoisement' of the American working class as factors limiting the development of socialism, have increasingly stressed that the awareness or perception of mobility is important as mobility itself in structuring social attitudes. In the words of S. Thermstrom: '. . . mobility data are meaningless except within a context of well defined attitudes and expectations about the class system . . .'[18] Thus the work of S. M. Lipset, R. Bendix, S. Thermstrom and others has pointed to the need to supplement empirical research on social mobility with a more inclusive analysis of the whole complex structure of American beliefs and value systems.

Finally, as different scholars have noted, one cannot fully understand how certain features of the American political system structure social development without relating them to the broader realm of American values and beliefs. The American Constitution is a case in point. Although the United States is certainly not the only modern nation–state with a Constitution, its uniqueness, in that for over two hundred years it has continued to be the central tenet of American values and institutions, distinguishes it from other constitutions, which have been changed and adapted by various political regimes. This, together with the 'sacredness' with which the American Constitution is imbued, has lent it its unique role in American life.

To sum up, it is evident that existing analyses have frequently indicated the fact that certain sociological and structural factors (open frontier, immigration, lack of a feudal past) though to some extent common to different societies, acquired special significance in America. Their unique constellation and coalescence with other symbolic elements and institutional arrangement lent America its 'exceptional' nature.

Americanism as an ideology

Clearly the role played by symbolic or ideological factors in defining the uniqueness of the American social order has not been limited to the problems of socialism; neither is it an especially new insight. Since the nineteenth century, and the writings of Alexis de Tocqueville and Lord Bryce, various attempts have been made to describe the uniqueness of America, as manifested both in the particular institutional mechanisms of American society and in its ideology.[19] In the course of his travels, it became clear to de Tocqueville that the 'laws and customs of American democracy' were maintained by a specific ideological structure rooted in a number of basic assumptions on the nature of man and society. These assumptions included a unique synthesis of the concepts of liberty and equality—which in Europe were viewed as antithetical, but in America were integrated in a novel structure—to become one of the defining characteristics of American thought. Through this singular integration, a pattern of social and political values, of normative criteria developed within American society in essence constituting the ideology of Americanism. Moreover, this social ideology was the focus of national identification in American nationalism.[20] The unique constellation of social ideology, national identity and individual adherence to theories and beliefs has rightly been seen as the major obstacle to the growth of socialist ideology in the United States.

From the different attempts to analyse the nature of American ideology, a number of effective lines of inquiry have been opened up, their differing foci representing some of the major themes within the complex structure of the American ideological system. These include:

(1) The particular components of the American 'civil religion' and its predominant value orientation;

(2) The messianic and millennial nature of the early American socio-political endeavour;

(3) Elements of disestablishmentarianism and 'liberty' as early institutional components of the American system;

(4) The particular components of solidarity and individualism, as opposed to collectivism, and the anti-statist orientations that evolved in American society;

(5) The particular structure of American nationalism, neither primordial nor rooted in organic historical development, with its unique ideological crystallisation;

(6) The strong future orientation of American values and beliefs;

(7) The existence of a constitutional concept of fundamental law. Rooted in medieval notions, this law was discovered by man but was not made by him, and serves to restrict human behaviour, positing norms of social action;

(8) The eighteenth century Enlightenment tradition of the social contract, natural rights, liberty, the limited role of government, the dependence of government on society and, of course, equality.

Basic components of the American civil religion

Robert Bellah noted that the American civil religion comprised a collection 'of beliefs', symbols and rituals with respect to sacred things '. . . a genuine apprehension of universal and transcendental religious reality as seen in or revealed through the experience of the American people.'[21] These institutionalised beliefs and rituals marked the parameters of the primary American value system. Its two major components were: (1) a unity of the English conception of natural law and that of 'higher law' drawn from Biblical religion, which formed the basis of legitimacy upon which the republic rested, and national identity was defined; and (2) the conception of religion as studiously non-denominational, resting on the broad Judeo–Christian traditions of Europe, and perceiving God to be intimately connected to and involved in American history and in the establishment of the American social order.

One of the factors which lent these components particular force was their integral connection to the broader fabric of what Bellah defined as the American 'Myth', through which historical experience is 'interpreted in light of transcendent reality,' that which 'seeks to transfigure reality so that it provides moral and spiritual meaning to individuals and societies.'[22] Through this mythical articulation of the historical process the political tenets noted above became woven into the fabric of the American civil religion. The following constitute additional strands of this ethos.

Origins

One of the major components of the American myth revolved around the origins, the 'newness', of America and the concomitant associations of pristine purity.[23] This is relevant on a number of levels: it tended to imbue the founding doctrines of American society with a certain 'sacredness' and also affected the American conception of history and the place of American and Americans therein, especially *vis-à-vis* Europe, as a symbol of the 'past'.[24] For the American conception of history was future-oriented, based on a radically new image of man 'emancipated from history'. The mythical importance of American newness was felt not only in the symbolism inscribed in its political and social consciousness; it stretched back in time to the first settlements and the European vision of America as the virgin new world, where man lived in a state of nature. America represented a primordial state of existence, related to the Biblical imagery of Eden and paradise. This, too, became an important element in the mythical significance of American origins.

The wilderness and rebirth

Inherent in this symbolic articulation of American origins, was a vision of man and nature instilled with Biblical images and symbols. The American wilderness was viewed either as the 'Promised Land', the 'New Canaan', 'paradise', or as Bellah noted, in a more Hobbesian light, evoking associations of an 'unfruitful desert, abode of death'. In either case, the image of the land was tied to a new paradigmatic image of man. The tension with the wilderness, the vision of its conquest together with man's own fall, reform and redemption, became a profound, dominant cultural idiom in American society.

Chosen people

A third focal point of the American myth was a firm belief that the American settlers were a 'chosen' people, with a mission (as noted by both de Tocqueville and Lord Bryce). Employing Biblical imagery to the full, the first Puritan settlers drew a symbolic parallel between themselves and the ancient Israelites. In so doing, they imposed, in Sacvan Bercovitz's words, a 'sacred *telos* on secular events'.[25] By the end of the eighteenth century, the destiny of the American republic was firmly identified with 'the course of redemptive history', America had become 'both the locus and instrument of the great consummation'.[26] The equation between the 'Kingdom of God' and the Nation, inherent in this belief and indeed, substituting this notion of the nation for the Church, became the central tenet of the 'religion of the republic'; so much so that 'the nation emerged as the primary agent of God's meaningful activity in history.'[27]

Messianism

These themes became concretised and their effects on social life were expressed in the seventeenth century colonial concept of the messianic nature of the American settlement. Through this vision, which played a crucial role in forming national consciousness, the individual and society were integrated in a unique scheme, that bound individual salvation to social responsibility and collective goals. This messianic idiom, which was inherent in the themes of chosenness and mission provided the medium through which unity between national and Biblical imagery could be articulated. This vision, rooted in early American historical development and in the socio-religious orientations of the Puritan settlers, constituted one of the focal points around which the particular American vision of man and society coalesced.

The messianic nature of the early American socio-political endeavour remained a recurrent theme in American history. In time, it was articulated as 'the light to the nations of the world' and provided an ideological framework for acts as disparate as the American Revolution and the Spanish-American War.

An even more significant contribution to the structuring of American consciousness was made through the unique configuration attained by the coalescence of eighteenth century English political theory with the Puritan ideas of being chosen, individualism and millennial expectations which stood at the root of the American civil religion.[28] The fusion of these diverse elements into an American messianic creed constituted an on-going theme in American social and political consciousness. It defined one of the basic parameters of national identity, structured collective goals and, as we shall see, its derivatives were crucial to the crystallisation of some of the major structural characteristics of American society (such as centre–periphery relations, structure of elites, and modes of protest articulation).

National identity and some socio-political derivatives of the American civil religion

The above discussed element which linked individual salvation to the accomplishments of the collective as a whole was central to American social and religious beliefs from the seventeenth century on. Sacvan Bercovitz noted 'The colonial Puritan myth linked self and social assertion in a way that lent special support to the American Way.'[29] The continual and successful articulation of this ideology rested on two crucial value orientations: a particular interpretation of individual fulfillment and the related value of equality. Rooted in pre-Revolutionary traditions of English radicalism, common law, natural rights and the Puritan value of the 'equality of believers', these orientations have been central to American life from the start and as, S. Lipset argued, the very legitimacy of the newly-founded republic rested upon them.[30] These orientations have, moreover, continued to characterise and inform American social life, and are constantly reapplied through the institutional orders of society.

An example of the method and dynamics of incorporation can be found in the interrelated themes of liberty-equality-protest and nation formation. The concept of equality, which drew heavily on that of English liberty for its political and religious legitimation, informed the ideological debate on both the separation from England and the crystallisation of an American national centre. Furthermore, from the mid-eighteenth century, the New England clergy drew increasingly strong parallels between civil and religious— or, in their terms, ecclesiastical—liberty, which were incorporated into the myth of American origins and the meaning of the Puritan settlement. In the eighteenth century, these aspects of liberty appeared threatened by England, depicted at the time as the 'Great Whore of Babylon' and identified with 'Papist slavery' and oppression. In the debates over English infringement of colonial rights, religious themes became interwoven with the 'conspiracy theories' then propagated by English radicals. Thus, during the revolutionary decades, the preservation of natural liberties became both justification for the Revolution and a virtue perceived as embodied only in the New World.[31]

A similar concern with liberty emerged from the intense religious strife engendered by the 'Great Awakening' of the 1740's. From the conflicts of '*Old*' and '*New Lights*', an interdependence between religious and political spheres emerged, leading to a degree of unity between the themes of individualism, religious morality and the concept of political liberties.[32] The derivatives of this development were felt in the spheres of protest and nation formation. For the sovereignty of the individual conscience, when united with the notions of political liberty and equality and imbued with religious sanctions, provided a potent legitimising force for protest. One of the results was the early legitimation and institutionalisation of protest in American society.

Concomitant with, and integral to the features mentioned above was the particular model of solidarity of membership in the American community—the terms of national identity. Just as a certain moral element was a constitutive factor in American politics, so were political factors a central focus of national identity. As an immigrant society of diverse religious faiths and divergent cultural backgrounds, the American conception of membership and collective identity has always been based on political ideals. The principles enumerated above, formulated with the founding of the political community, have been viewed as the binding principles of collective life ever since. Thus, adherence to these principles, to the codes of the civil religion and political ideals articulated and instituted with the republic, defines the parameters of American collective identity. Throughout history, being American has been equated with believing in this civil religion. With this essentially political criterion for membership and integration into the community, it is not surprising that alternative political creeds have been able to make little headway in American society and culture. The crux of the argument regarding the immigrants' desire be integrated and adapt to the prevailing value system lies, therefore, not only in them, but in the demands of the system, which posited the adoption of a particular political-religious creed as the criterion for acceptance.

Two other characteristics of the American socio-political creed have been indicated as relevant to analysis of the American ideological structure: the individualism and the strong anti-statist political attitudes of Americans. The crystallisation of American nationalism, in effect, witnessed the transformation of the European concept of individualism, as its original negative associations metamorphosised into political virtues. Indeed, it was through the unique American articulation of the doctrine of individualism that the 'European' contradiction between liberty and equality was resolved. The individualism which de Tocqueville viewed negatively as the expression of an *atomised* society, was re-articulated in America along different lines, drawing on indigenous American traditions. Since the early days of settlement, republican liberties had been viewed as correlates of the Puritan tradition, based as it was on the individual and his freedom of conscience. To this the early nineteenth century transcendentalists and Unitarians added their vision of the perfectibility of man, based on the growth of enlightenment and education. In the words of Y. Arieli: 'Individuality, liberty and self-government were the main vehicles in the progress toward perfection'.[33] A new concept of the individual and individualism was articulated, in the works of W. E. Channing, Garisson, Thoreau and Emerson: 'The rights of man and democracy were the political expressions of religious and philosophical truth . . . aimed at the vindication of the greatness of man in each individual.'[34] Together, these doctrines formed a crucial component of American national consciousness and of its central value system.

Symbolic premises of the American centre and major characteristics of the institutional structure

Based on the different ideological elements reviewed in the preceding pages, various attempts have been made to relate ideological and structural spheres in an analysis of the American social system. From our study of the different factors comprising the American civil religion, a number of elements stand out as particularly relevant to understanding the crystallisation of dominant American socio-political orientations. Some of these were shared by all societies participating in the Judeo–Christian tradition; others were more pronounced within Reformation societies; while others still were related to the developments of dissenting Protestantism specific to America. Among the most important were the following:[35]

(1) the high degree of transcendental tension between the cosmic and mundane orders and the extensive interweaving of this-wordly and other-wordly modes of salvation (of bridging the chasm, with a marked emphasis on this-worldly activities). The derivatives of this orientation in such fields as the soteriological meaning attributed to economic activity, the entrepeneur as cultural hero, the idealisation of the political sphere, America's millennial role, and the high level of collective participation in and responsibility to political and cultural orders, were crucial factors in structuring the American social and political orders.

(2) The high level of individual commitment to the cosmic and mundane centres, enshrined in the founding of all Puritan communities

and related to the strong perception of the messianic nature of the colonial endeavour and convenanted nature of the original Puritan collective.

(3) The orientation towards direct access to both cosmic and mundane centres. In contrast to the mediated nature of access to the transcendental centre found in Catholic religious orientations, American Puritanism stressed the direct, autonomous and unmediated access of the individual to the transcendental centre. Through the process of mutural impingement of conflicting religious elites, this orientation achieved social relevance and was given political articulation in the form of direct access to the mundane centre.[36]

(4) Out of the original Puritan doctrine of 'equality of believers' emerged yet another crucial cultural orientation—towards social equality and against the development of ascriptive criteria for access to power or prestige, or membership in the collective.

(5) Another orientation was in the realm of collective identity founded on the concept of convenanted community. This doctrine, central to the development of both American nationalism and individualism, precluded the type of primordial ascriptive criteria for membership characteristic of European societies, and constituted relatively well defined boundaries of identification and parameters of collective identity.

Thus, while collective membership was based on acceptance of certain fundamental principles, its religious character being transformed with time, it theoretically remained open and contained none of the a priori exclusionary criteria characterstic in Europe. This *'sacralisation'* of the community, one of the constitutive elements in the formation of collective (and later national) identity, left little room for adopting alternative models of identification; it mitigated against an individual's motivation towards goals viewed as beyond the parameters of the American way of life and tended to consider those so motivated to be outside the 'normative societal community'.[37] To fully appreciate the importance of the above mentioned orientations in the organisation of social life, it is necessary to examine their institutional embodiments in the structure of the American centre and its elite groups.

American centre[38]

The American centre manifested a number of unique characteristics, both symbolic and structural in nature; together, these tended to define its uniqueness and to contribute to the particular course taken in America by protest impingement and centre response.

Symbolic premises

On the symbolic level, the following represent some of the most critical defining traits of the American centre:

— Its principal defining trait was openness. Symbolically, the centre bore no differentiation from the periphery and was seen as embracing the whole collective.

— The particular symbolic and institutional set of relationships between Church and State was at the root of many of the unique characteristics of the American social order. The early separation of powers was nevertheless concomitant with the continuation of a deep religious tone or theme within the political sphere. As opposed to many modern secular centres, the separation between Church and State in America did not engender the type of virulent anticlericalism that characterized social centres and societies emerging from the traditional social order.

— In the years following the Revolution, there emerged in the United States a legal rational system of legitimation. Although the figure of Washington was originally imbued with a high degree of charisma, this charisma quickly became institutionalised and lost its personal attributes. This fact, with its derivative in the realms of full franchise, and granting of legitimation to protest movements and elites, was enforced by orientations towards achievement and equality and stood at the centre of the American sociopolitical consensus.

Structural characteristics

Following the symbolic attributes were a number of structural characteristics which, while serving to define centre–perphery relations, had a crucial impact on the development of protest in America. Among the organisational features of the American centre and social order, the most relevant to our problem were found to be:

(1) The particular structure of institutional mechanisms of access, allowing direct and unmediated access to centre orders by all members of the collective. (Significant exceptions to their workings were of course the cases of slavery and the mediated nature of the legitimation granted to working class organisation. In both cases,

economic interests as well as the particular orientations towards collective identity and the boundaries of accepted social practice were factors in the bitterness of the conflict and the propensity to view certain individuals and forms of social action as beyond the accepted parameters of the 'American way of life'.)

(2) The primary organisational nature of the problems facing the centre. In contrast to Europe, where the two focal points of social conflict in the early periods of nation formation tended to be the legitimation of political power and the crystallisation of collective identity, in America these issues were resolved before the crystallisation of the political centre. As a result, the basic problems of the American centre were organisational and regulatory in nature, in marked contrast to other nation–state centres whose primary task lay in restructuring and redefining the ideological parameters of social life.[39]

There were a number of important derivatives of the above in the sphere of protest. They engendered a high degree of commitment to the social and political orders, thereby affecting the trajectory taken by protest, which could not successfully impinge on the basic tenets of the social order, as it did in Europe (where the definitive crystallisation of modes of political legitimacy and models of collective identity continued to be the *loci* of protest).

Another important influence was on the integrative powers of the centre. Territorial expansion never engendered the development of competing sub-centres or alternative *loci* of power and allegiance. The integrative capacity of the centre affected also the expression and political articulation of social tensions.

One of the critical results of the early crystallisation of the symbolic and structural arrangements noted above was in the establishment of some relatively well-defined ground rules of social interaction, whose saliency was maintained throughout the historical trajectory of American development. Their importance was felt primarily in times of crisis, stress and social and economic restructuring and dislocation. For whatever social tensions and violence which cut across American history, these ground rules successfully maintained a set of ideological and institutional parameters within which tensions and conflicts could be met and resolved. Thus, though the nature and saliency of the conflicts changed in the course of American history, the early frameworks and institutional boundaries remained constant features of American life. The structures of American federalism, the Constitution, the importance of individual political leaders (as opposed to parties), were all developments which ensured the continuity of such parameters and consensual norms, despite high levels of tension. An additional factor in this dynamic was found to be the structure of American elite groups, who played a major role in the continuity of the early institutional frameworks of social interaction.

Major characteristics of American elites

The different elite groups shared certain symbolic assumptions and organisational characteristics which proved crucial to the development of American socialism.

The most important of the major symbolic assumptions were the unrestricted potentiality of all social actors to become elites and of different elite structures to articulate orientations in all spheres of social life; the interweaving of orientations between different elite groups; unlike Europe, no segregation of orientations among elites existed; and the fact that carriers of orientations in all spheres of social life (legal, economic, social and religious) were accepted as legitimate articulators of social models and desiderata.

The symbolic assumptions on the nature of American elites reflected certain aspects of their organisational characteristics. A number of these were predominant from early crystallisation of the American centre:

— Their autonomous nature: they were relatively free of rigid social structures and frameworks. This was true of religious, intellectual, entrepreneurial and political elites.
— The relative weakness of elite specialisation: this was related both to the interweaving of orientations and to the symbolic lack of differentiation between elites. Although there was some degree of specialisation among entrepreneurial elites, it was importantly, lacking among political elites.
— The extensive structural weakness and lack of organisational strength among elites, especially political elites. As a result, only temporary coalitions between elite groups were formed—a factor which was essential in ensuring the continued functioning of democracy within the American socio-political system. The competition between elites which led to the search for general support among broader groups in the collective, resulted in what Lipset has termed 'institutionalised conflict'—conflict whose parameters were determined by the consensus on values shared within the collective. This influenced the development of a framework in which protest could

be articulated and incorporated without the destructive dislocation of the system as a whole.
— Finally, no clear distinction existed between centre and periphery elites. Thus, though differences of power and prestige clearly existed, they did not determine the inclusion or exclusion of elites from participation in or articulation of major facets of social life. The different elites maintained close institutional ties with central structures and orders, while retaining their autonomy.

The preceding review of the symbolic and structural characteristics of the American system offers new insights into some of the social and political factors presented hitherto as relevant to the failure of American socialism. For it can be argued that these characteristics of American social life and ideology played an important role in structuring some of the basic variables used in the study of class politics and modes of protest: the struggle for the franchise, for working class membership in collective life, and for legitimation of working class political and economic organisations. In the following we shall show the interrelation of the above themes as they effected the dynamics of socialism in America.

Americanism, protest and socialism

Protest and civil religion

The inability of political protest to become successfully organised in the framework of a third party has been widely analysed as a phenomenon of American life. It has been related to various factors, including the constitutionally entrenched two-party system, the nature of American federalism and the flexibility of American coalition politics. These factors in turn have been related to the nature of the American centre, its value orientations and the characteristics of American elite groups—characteristics which defined American political culture and were important in structuring the modes of protest which developed in American society. S. Lipset observed that 'movements not parties' have been 'the American response to social crisis, to failures in the two party system.'[40] He relates this to the 'Protestant' character of the United States, with its emphasis on individual morality, and points to what has, in fact, been our major problem: the effect of the different ideological and orientational factors, as carried by different social elites, on structuring the specific dynamics of protest impingement and response in America.

Protest, no less than society's fundamental symbolic and institutional orders, was profoundly influenced by the orientational perspectives, religious tenets and value assumption which crystallised among the early Puritan settlers. Sharing the same fundamental symbolic tenets, protest in America was intimately related to what has been termed the American 'civil religion'. It shared its messianic conceptions, its notions of individual moral accountability and responsibility, the basic commitment to the social order and, of course, the demand for greater equality. American traditions of protest were thus characterised by a tendency to reaffirm 'traditional American values', specifically liberty, equality and popular control over, and participation in, government. Protest tended to be 'reformist' in character, oriented towards the increased institutional implementation of centre symbolism.

Sharing the symbolic premises of society as a whole, and of its centre, protest movements never articulated alternative *loci* of values, norms or collective identity beyond the parameters of the American belief system. On the organisational level, protest was characterised by a relatively high degree of incorporation, lack of specialisation and organisational weakness among its elites and indeed, by a high degree of orientational continuity and organisational discontinuity.

These features, together with the legitimacy granted to protest and the incorporation of its tenets into the basic institutional and symbolic orders of the centre gave rise to the particular characteristics of protest and protest incorporation. Protest movements which impinged strongly on the centre when concerned with a local or specific issue, tended to loose their saliency when forced to compete on a national level and address themselves to a myriad of issues which, when taken together, were conceived in America as constituting not only a political but a moral creed. In the move from concrete issues to broader assumptions regarding the working of the socio-political order—one set of these assumptions which was firmly entrenched in the very definition of the national–collective—protesting elites either fell back on the dominant ideological symbolic structure (and its institutional derivatives), or articulated an alternative conception of the social order (with devastating results, as for Calhoun or Debbs).

The need to broaden the issues and constitute a wider platform in order to mobilise support, the ultimate failure to do so and, at the same time, the incorporation of major elements of protest demands by the existing parties, have all been constant features of the dynamics of protest in America. The case of the Populists and their failure to transcend the free silver issue is a case in point, as was the more recent failure of the New Left in the 1960s to mobilise support for collective goals and desiderata beyond the end of the Vietnam War, (or to articulate a consistent theoretical position, a failure they shared with the 'old-left'). Moreover, the protesting elites' use of both the existing organisational and institutional mechanisms and the dominant ideological assumptions gave protest its characteristic features as a reform movement within the existing political structures, rather than permitting the crystallisation of competing party structures.

The organisational weakness of American protest is only enhanced when placed in a comparative perspective. All protest movements in Europe, whether prior to or during the industrialisation process, found their modes of access to the centre, political participation, and organisational growth blocked by the dominant political powers. This led to the crystallisation of alternative ideological systems embracing central symbolic tenets beyond immediate concrete demands and needs. These movements' organisational strength often lay in their ability to unite concrete demands (for equality, access, participation, organisational and political freedom), with a broader ideological construct, which often drew on past traditions, on the continuity of older foci of identity and resistance.[41] In America there was no rationale for the existence of such symbolic and organisational structures because of the very nature of the centre, and the legitimacy and autonomy granted to all groups of political elites.

Socialism

In its underlying orientations, structural characteristics and modes of impingement, the American socialist movement shared many of the traits common to American protest movements. The reason for its failure to develop along similar lines to European socialist movements is to be sought both in these factors, as well as in the unique coalescence of structural and symbolic orders which characterised the American centre. The same mechanisms which played a role in absorbing earlier forms of protest and limiting their crystallisation into powerful social and ideological systems were instrumental in hampering the growth of socialism in the United States.

On the symbolic level, American socialism shared many of the basic premises of society as a whole: its strong future orientation, messianism, this-worldliness, emphasis on active participation and commitment to the social order. It was, in fact, the fundamental affinity between the major symbolic assumptions of the American ideological system and the socialist movement that led the socialist Leo Sampson, to define 'Americanism' as a 'surrogate socialism'.[42] This shared symbolism influenced socialist development in three ways:

— It militated against the development of a strong ideological system capable of mobilising mass support, since it offered nothing fundamentally new to American social values.
— It tended, through the 'moralism' of the movement, to place socialism within a well-defined tradition of American protest, within the established pattern of impingement and response—a pattern which led to the increased 'moral awareness' of large segments of the population. This 'awareness', however, was channeled into existing social and political structures (such as the Democratic Party).
— Sharing the same fundamental assumptions as the established social order, as well as the traditions of morally articulated protest, socialists tended to focus their debate on 'bread and butter' issues, rather than to develop a fully articulated theoretical or ideological position.

Beyond those symbolic assumptions shared by the social centre and American socialists, there were additional features of the ideology of Americanism that stood in direct opposition to socialist ideology. The most important of these was the nature of American nationalism and collective identity, which went beyond a mere loyalty to the State.[43] The sovereignty of the individual conscience, the principles of political activity, commitment and responsibility to the social and cosmic order, were given a quasi-religious articulation (the 'civil religion'), and infused the doctrine of American nationalism. These parameters of national identification, embodying as they did specific political structures and organisational frameworks, not only stood in opposition to socialist universal and collective orientations, but also limited the crystallisation of alternative foci of identification and political mobilisation.

Another organisational factor in the above dynamic was the lack of specialisation and the heterogeneity of the elites, which led to a high degree of inter-penetration of socialist and trade union activists (especially in the years 1912–20). While this facilitated temporary influence within the unions, the ultimate result was to drain leadership cadres from the socialist movement (particularly after the break-up of their national organisation in 1920). The political failure of the socialists led many of those who had been trained in organisational abilities within the movement to drop their party affiliation and concentrate on union organisation.

Similarly, the potential of all social actors to become elites and the institutional channels of access open to them, tended to isolate the socialists from the broader dimensions of the political process. Special interests and demands were articulated by different structures of elites and did not require the intervention of any specific political organisation. Moreover, no special interest group relied on socialist electoral success to implement their demands. A good example of this dynamic can be found in the relation of American trade unionism to socialism, especially when viewed from a comparative perspective.

One of the most notable failures of American socialism has been its inability to mobilise support from among the industrial working class, while the unions succeeded in representing their demands and found a place within the corporate structure of American society. These characteristics in particular invite an analysis of working class and union integration not limited to a study of the unions themselves, but relating the characteristics of union activity to the dominant social structure upon which it impinged. This indeed was the focus of S. M. Lipset's study, whose major findings deal with the degree of working class integration into society as a whole, and the *de jure* and *de facto* legitimation granted union organisation.[44] The case of France, where *de jure* recognition of trade union activities existed, but *de facto* acceptance of working class rights did not, is a good case for comparison: despite the legal sanction, the 'business classes' of France continually sought to break the unions and suppress the working class. They refused to adhere to collective bargaining agreements and often successfully sabotaged the administration of reform legislation designed to improve the conditions of labour or raise wages'.[45] As a result, socialist and syndicalist ideology was predominant among French trade unionists. In America, by contrast, the notions of participation, open access to the centre, commitment to the social order and equality tended to inform the attitudes of both workers and employers and to structure their social interaction.

A particularly instructive example of this can be seen in attitudes towards collective bargaining. For, while it was the American unions' strength that brought the 'business classes' to the bargaining table, the ensuing cooperation of labour with managerial classes was not a foregone conclusion—as the contrasting cases of France and other countries make clear. Rather, the major cultural orientations and symbolic assumptions, shared by both labour and management, made collective bargaining the type of institutional structure it was. The acceptance and integration of the working class into the decision-making process, and its participation in social construction, affected working class politics and ideology to no small extent. Within labour, as in management, the specific cultural orientations unique to America endowed collective bargaining with its particular dynamic. This point was made by Paul Jacobs and is among Laslett's findings in his study of American unions which show how labour's acceptance of negotiated contracts implied recognition of its responsibilities to the social order and a rejection of radical tactics.[46]

Here, too, the difference between Europe and America is evident. In European societies, where class barriers were not only economic, but also defined by traditional status assumptions, there developed no necessary conflicts between collective bargaining and the revolutionary assumptions of socialism'.[47] In America, working class acceptance of the predominant social values was not solely the outcome of its unique mobility and class fluidity. The fact that even the most radical trade unionists came to recognise a contradiction between revolutionary socialism and the collective bargaining process points to the importance of shared cultural and symbolic elements and their role in modifying notions of class and class politics. Moreover, the significance of these developments lies in showing how the working class was brought into society, through participation in decision-making, access to the centre, and a greater share in society's resources, thereby making them it 'of the centre' as well as 'in it'.

Conclusion

In relating the specific characteristics of American socialism to some of the major symbolic and organisational aspects of the American social order, this research has attempted to broaden the perspectives opened by past analysis, not only of American socialism but of comparative modes of protest in general. It has become clear through this analysis that the case for American uniqueness must be made while taking close account of the particular articulation within American society of some of the major symbolic dimensions of collective existence and their institutional expression in the social order. These major dimensions, which we attempted to codify in a number of socio-cultural orientations, achieved a unique constellation in America—one which united with the specific characteristics of American elites, contributed to the major distinctive features of the social centre and to the particular articulation and incorporation of protest in America. As comparative work has shown, there are many elements of American social development which are not unique: parallels and corollaries with other societies did and still do exist. What was unique, however, was the particular pattern of major cultural orientations, the characteristics of the elite groups carrying them, and the modes of their institutionalisation in the central orders of society. Thus, as we have seen the early religious orientations, their mode of application to the socio-cultural and political spheres and consequent role in structuring status notions, collective solidarity and the granting of political rights and liberties all played an important role in informing the American experience of socialist impingement and centre response.

Notes

1. W. Sombart, *Why Is There No Socialism in the U.S.A.*, London, Macmilliam Press, 1975.
2. The following characterisation draws mainly from the following: J. Laslett and S. M. Lipset, (eds.), *Failure of A Dream*, New York, Anchor Books, 1974; J. Laslett, *Labour and the Left*, New York, Basic Books, 1970; P. Foner, *History of the Labor Movement in the U.S.A.*, New York International Publishers, 1947–1965; C. Lash, *The Agony of the American Left*, New York, A. Knopf, 1969; J. Weinstein, *The Decline of Socialism in the U.S.A.*, New York, Monthly Review Press, 1967; C. Shannon, *Socialist Party of America*, New York, Macmillan, 1955.
3. D. Bell, 'The Background and the Development of Marxian Socialism in the United States', in D. Egbert and S. Persons, *Socialism and American Life*, Princeton, Princeton University Press, 1952, pp. 213–405.
4. See L Hartz, *The Liberal Tradition in America*, New York, Harcourt Brace and Co., 1955.
5. See Laslett and Lipset, *Failure of a Dream*.
6. See K. Mayer, 'Social Structure in Two Equalitarian Societies: Australia and the U.S.A.', in S. M. Lipset and B. Bendix, (eds.), *Class Status and Power*, (2nd edition), Glencoe, Free Press, 1966, pp. 149–61.
7. See Sombart, *Why There Is No Socialism*, esp. pp. 115–16.
8. S. Thernstrom, 'Socialism and Social Mobility', in Laslett and Lipset, *Failure of a Dream*, p. 524.
9. S. M. Lipset and B. Bendix, *Social Mobility in Industrial Society*, Berkeley, University of California Press, 1960.
10. See S. M. Lipset, 'American Exceptionalism in the North American Perspective: Why the United States has withstood the World Socialist Movement', in G. M. Adams, (ed.), *The Idea of America*, Cambridge, Harvard University Press, 1977.
11. See S. M. Lipset, 'American Exceptionalism', in M. Novak, *Capitalism and Socialism: A Theological Inquiry*, Washington, D.C., A.E. 1, 1979, pp. 34–60.

12. See M. Robin, *Radical Politics and Canadian Labor 1880—1930*, cited in Lipset, 'American Exceptionalism'.

13. See B. Fitzpatrick, 'The Big Man's Frontier', in *Agricultural History*, XXI, 1947, pp. 8–12; F. Alexander, *Moving Frontiers: An American Theme and its Application to Australian History*, Melbourne, Melbourne University Press, 1947; P. A. Sharp, 'Three Frontiers: Some Comparative Studies of Canadian, American and Australian Settlement, *Pacific Historical Review*, **24**, 1955; P. J. Coleman, 'The New Zealand Frontier and the Turner Thesis, *Pacific Historical Review*, **27**, 1958, pp. 221–37; Hofstadter, R. and Lipset, S. M., *Turner and the Sociology of the Frontier*, N. Y., Basic Books, 1968.

14. See Laslett, *Labor and the Left*.

15. See Hartz, *The Liberal Tradition*.

16. See Mayer, 'Social Structure'.

17. See Lipset, 'American Exceptionalism', 1977.

18. See Thernstrom, 'Socialism', p. 550.

19. See A. de Tocqueville, *Democracy in America*, N.Y., A. Knopf, 1946 and J. Bryce, *The American Commonwealth*, London, Macmillan, 1981.

20. See Y. Arieli, *Individualism and Nationalism in American Ideology*, Cambridge, Harvard University Press, 1964.

21. R. Bellah, 'On Civil Religion in America', in *Daedalus*, Winter, 1967, p. 12.

22. R. Bellah, *The Broken Covenant*, New York, Seabury Press, 1975, p. 3.

23. See Arieli, *Individualism*; Bellah, 'Civil Religion'.

24. See Bellah, 'Civil Religion' and R. W. B. Lewis, *The American Adam*, Chicago, University of Chicago Press, 1955.

25. S. Bercovitch, *The Puritan Origins of the American Self*, New Haven, Yale University Press, 1975, p. 52.

26. See J. MacClear, 'The Republic and the Millenium', in E. Smith, ed., *The Religion of the Republic*, Philadelphia, Fordstea Press, 1971, pp. 183–216; J. G. A. Pocock, *The Machiavellian Moment*, Princeton, Princeton University Press, 1975; R. L. Tuveson, *Redeemer Nation: The Idea of America's Millennial Role*, Chicago, University of Chicago Press, 1968. For a general, if somewhat dated, review of the relevant literature, see D. Smith, 'Millennial Scholarship in America', *American Quarterly*, **17**, 1965, pp. 535–49.

27. See N. O. Hatch, *The Sacred Cause of Liberty*, New Haven, Yale University Presss, 1977; R. M. Bloch, *Visionary Millennial Themes in American Thought 1756—1800*, N. Y., Cambridge University Press, 1985.

28. See B. Bailyn, *The Ideological Origins of the American Revolution*, Cambridge, Harvard University Press, 1982.

29. S. Bercovitch, *The Puritan Origins*, p. 185.

30. See S. M. Lipset, *The First New Nation*, London, Heineman, 1963.

31. See Hatch, *The Sacred Cause*; and Bailyn, *The Ideological Origins*.

32. See A. Heimart, *Religion and the American Mind*, Cambridge, Harvard University Press, 1966.

33. Y. Arieli, *Individualism*, p. 272.

34. *Ibid.*
35. See the introductory chapter of this book for greater elaboration of these themes.
36. For more on these perspectives see S. N. Eisenstadt, *The Protestant Ethic and Modernization*, New York, Basic Books, 1968; and his *Revolutions and Transformations of Societies*, New York, Free Press, 1978.
37. See E. Tiryakin, 'Puritan America in the Modern World: Mission Impossible', Durham, North Carolina, 1982.
38. For the sociological use of the concept, 'centre', see E. Shils, *Centre and Periphery: Essays in Macrosociology*, Chicago, University of Chicago Press, 1975.
39. See Lipset, *The First New Nation*.
40. Lipset, 'American Exceptionalism', 1977.
41. See S. Rokkan, (ed.), *Comparative Research Across Cultures and Nations*, Paris, Maton, 1968; S. Rokkan and S. N. Eisenstadt, *Building States and Nations*, Beverly Hills, Sage Publications, 1973.
42. L. Sampson, in Laslett and Lipset, *Failure of a Dream*, p. 426.
43. The concept of the State does not appear in American political discourse, in contrast with the 'classical' European distinction between 'State' and 'Civil Society'. Likewise, more primordial forms of collective solidarity existing in Europe did not exist in America. The integration of the Jew, no less than the working-class, into the social and political life of the community was an important derivative of this latter feature.
44. S. M. Lipset, 'Radicalism or Reformism: The Sources of Working Class Politics', address presented at the American Political Science Annual Meeting, 2.9.82, Denver, CO.
45. *Ibid.*, p. 43.
46. See Laslett, *Labor and the Left*.
47. *Ibid.*, p. 301.

Part II: Centres and social stratification in Europe and the United States

The structuring of social hierarchies in comparative perspective

S. N. Eisenstadt

Analytical problems in earlier studies of stratification

In this section we would like to throw some new light on the structuring of social hierarchies paying special attention to the role of ideas in this process. We shall begin by making a critical evaluation of the basic assumptions of sociological studies in this field. Assumptions which are shared to some degree by both the Marxists and 'liberal' approaches to the problem of class formation.[1]

Most of these studies have assumed that the major dimensions of social hierarchies are structured by the level of development of technology and structural differentiation and in Marxist views also by the modes of production, that is by the forces which shape the structure of the social division of labour in society.[2] These dimensions of social hierarchies are: (1) their group basis (whether occupational, regional, ethnic and the like), which form the basic units of stratification; (2) the principles or criteria of such structuring (of differential evaluation of different position); (3) the structuring of status or class consciousness and of perception of class interests, class conflicts; and (4) the concrete patterns of stratification (e.g. the relative predominance of vertical or horizontal formations).

In the discussions and controversies regarding the analysis of stratification, a continuous emphasis was placed on the importance of power elements in the structuring of social hierarchies and class formations. On the whole however, there was little systematic explication of the relation between such power elements and the structuring of the social division of labour. One could develop the impression that these power elements were in a sense just constitutive parts of such division of labour and of the conflicts of interests they give rise to.

In fact, the Marxist concept of modes of production as connected to the structure of power between social groups in a class formation goes beyond a simple emphasis on technology and structural differentiation, but this potential insight was rarely explicated in the literature. Moreover, most of these studies have assumed that the crystallisation of strata or classes (whether viewed in Marxist terms of power or Weberian terms of life chances), as well as their inherent conflicts, is correlated with the development of a market economy, of industrial societies in general and of capitalism in particular, and with growing—even if only symbolic—political modernisation.

These studies have also assumed that such crystallisation takes place through the development of a high degree of country-wide strata (class) consciousness. This tends to minimise the important of ethnic, religious or regional groups and is characterised by a high degree of status association and perception of common class interests, an autonomous access to those social and cultural attributes which serve as bases and criteria of status, and a high degree of political articulation and expression of respective class interests and conflicts.

A critical examination of these assumptions can shed light on the problem of the determinants which structure social hierarchies and class formations. Such an analysis may also shed light on a closely connected problem of central interest from the point of view of sociological theory, namely that of the conditions which influence the modes of perception, articulation and organisation of interests in human interaction in general and of class interests in particular.

Explanations of social behaviour and organisation in terms of ideas (or values) or of interests (or power) have often been conceived as mutually exclusive, almost totally irreconcilable, as being based on entirely different conceptions of man, of social action and of social order. For instance, Seymour Lipset has stated that 'the focus of functionalists on values as distinct from interests seems to the critics to result in an underestimation of the inherent forces for social conflict among those having different interests.'[3] These contrasting approaches have been revived in recent sociological controversies in general and in the different approaches of Marxists and structuralists in particular.

Although one of the founding fathers of sociology, Max Weber, recognised the importance of ideas in structuring class interests, subsequent sociological analyses have not gone beyond general insights nor tried to specify in a systematic way the possible connections between ideas and interests.[4] It would be useful to state explicitly which are the ideas that influence central aspects of the social structure and the definition and perception of specific interests in sociology, and to understand the processes through which such influence structures social action and what is the place of power in these social dynamics.

We hope that a critical analysis of the determinants of class formation and the structuring of social hierarchies might also throw some light on this central problem of sociological analysis.

The prevailing analytic outlook on social stratification owes much to the Western European configuration. In Western Europe and to a lesser degree in the Byzantine Empire, the criteria of status were usually based on the proximity of individuals to some general cultural (religious) or social attributes, functional service to society, as well as relative standing with respect to wealth and power.[5]

The European class structure was based on the fact that many classes and especially the free ones, had relatively autonomous access to such major attributes of the cosmic and social order from which presumably the criteria of status were derived. Hence, most groups could participate in the centre by virtue of their collective identities, as corporate or semi-corporate bodies, and a countrywide 'consciousness' or organisation developed that was not confined to the higher groups, but could also be found among the 'middle' or lowest free groups and stata.

In a parallel manner there developed in Western Europe a rather strong tendency toward the predominance of broad occupational definitions of class, that is of each stratum tending to encompass a great variety of occupational positions and organisations and to link them in some common way of life, resulting in a high degree of broad status association as opposed to status segregation.

A strong tendency developed toward a relatively broad class consciousness and toward the definition of class conflicts in broad terms. This was especially evident among the higher strata, but it certainly was not unknown among the middle and even the lower free strata. The fullest expression of this tendency was to be found in the system of representation in the various assemblies of estates whose roots go back to the possibility of political participation in the centre which was available to most groups, by virtue of their identities as corporate or semicorporate bodies. Many of those characteristics of the European class structure can be also discerned in modern times.[6]

As one contrasts Western Europe with other historical societies evincing similar levels of social, structural and technological differentiation and similar forms of division of labour, far-reaching differences appear in all the major dimensions of structuring of social hierarchies mentioned above. Namely those connected to the group basis of such structuring, the perception of class of strata consciousness and the forms of articulation of class interests, activities as well as the forms of political expression of such strata consciousness.

Thus for instance in the Chinese Empire[7] there developed a relatively clear ideological evaluation of different occupational positions, based on their proximity to the basic tenets of the Confucian order. The official picture of society enshrined in the Confucian ideology was complemented by a strong normative definition of the style of life and collective identity of different social strata. The *literati* and to some extent the gentry had the highest prestige followed by the peasants. The merchants and the military had less, and vagabounds, entertainers and beggars had the least. The highest groups (the *literati* and the bureaucracy) developed a relatively high degree of country-wide class consciousness and solidarity rooted in a common cultural tradition—the sharing of common avenues of access to central positions and the fact that these avenues, the schools and the academies, were to some extent independent of the centre although oriented to it. These characteristics of country wide consciousness and solidarity were attenuated by the existence of more local, peripheral attributes of status. On this local level family and lineage groups served as main agents of socialisation and cultivated distinct styles of life. Kinship units were highly important in determining family status and the possibility of gaining access to the centre, although these were never fully legitimised nor automatic. Similarly a society-wide consciousness and potential class orientation to conflict did not develop among the merchants, other urban groups or the peasantry.

In both Czarist and Soviet Russia[8] there developed some tendencies seemingly similar to those discernible in Europe, but these were counteracted by the strong attempts of the ruling elites to emphasise functional contributions to the welfare of society as defined by the centre, to minimise the autonomous expression of class consciousness and to segregate different occupational and social groups which might have coalesced into broader horizontal statuses. The group basis of social hierarchies continuously oscillated between a tendency to such relatively broad, territorial and occupational bases rooted in the common European experience and a *de facto*, much narrowwer scope characterised by the policies of the central elites. The rulers of both Czarist and modern Soviet Russia tended to encourage segregation of lifestyles and patterns of participation among different local, occupational, and territorial kinship groups. They attempted to minimize the 'status' or 'class' components of family or kinship groups identity as well as the autonomous standing of the family in the status system and aimed to discourage the development of autonomous, countrywide class consciousness in general and a political expression of such consciousness, conflict and organisation in particular.

The structuring of social hierarchies in many Middle Eastern societies (here the best comparison would be between some 'traditional' Middle Eastern Empires, such as the Abbaside or Ottoman ones and other agrarian empires) exhibits again specific characteristics.[9] A multiplicity of status-groups—ethnic, religious, local, regional, sectorial or tribal—developed with a high degree of status segregation among them. The major criteria of status were family membership and proximity to the basic attributes of the social and religious order, but these attributes were to a very large degree controlled by the major political and religious centres of these societies, which minimised the autonomous access of different status units to such controlling positions, as well as to some degree, to the major attributes of status. The combination of these principles of structuring of hierarchies with the group basis of such hierarchies generated a tendency according to which 'service aristocracies' and bureaucracies developed as the apex of higher classes and as channels of social mobility, sharpening the division between the upper groups in the centre and the wider groups on the periphery, for the status sets and units to be arranged vertically rather than horizontally.

The foregoing, brief contrast between Western Europe and other societies indicates that similar structures of division of labour can be combined with different conceptions of class interests and activities and different political expressions of strata and class consciousness. Differences existed in the above societies with respect to the structuring of concrete patterns of stratification and conflict and especially in the extent to which hierarchical structuring was focused on cross-cutting network and vertical commitments or in horizontal, broad and autonomous class formations.

Accordingly the existence of these complex differences cannot be explained solely in terms of the levels and types of resources generated by different technologies or by structural differentiation and modes of production, that is, by the structure of social division of labour that developed in these societies. The societies studied here, with all the differences between them, showed rather striking similarities in these respects.[10] We would like instead to propose that the structuring of these aspects of social hierarchies is greatly influenced by different modes of control over the production flow of the basic resources generated by the social division of labour, control which is exercised by special social actors and in which power and ideological components are very strongly interwoven.

Elites as controllers of information and resources

The starting point of our analysis has to be the identification of the social actors and mechanisms through which such control over the production and flow of resources was exercised. Obviously, it would not do to talk of 'class' as such an actor, since it is exactly the differences in the structuring of seemingly similar class interests that constitute the major problem of our analysis. Instead, we suggest that it would be best to follow Weber and even some ideas implicit in Marx's analysis (or some Marxists like Gramsci[11]) which have indicated that the crucial elements in the structuring of such formations and interests seem to be the major elite or institutional entrepreneurs, especially political and cultural elites, or, in more technical terms, the articulators of models of the social order.

There were, however, important differences within the above noted societies both with respect to the orientations their elites carried and with respect to the organisational structure of these elites. They varied first of all with respect to the strength of the perception of the tension between the cosmic and mundane worlds; and secondly, with respect to the relative emphasis on a purely this-wordly mode of salvation (as in China), on a purely other-worldly mode of salvation (as in Hinduism and Buddhism), or on some interconnection between them (as in the monotheistic civilisations). Among those societies emphasising the interconnection of this-wordly and other-worldly salvation, there were variations with respect to the degree of the interweaving or segregation of this-worldly and other-worldly foci of salvation (a problem that is inherent in most high civilisations and religions), as well as with respect to the specification of the institutional arenas of such salvation.

Beyond this, there were important differences in these societies with respect to the degree to which the primordial collectivities were seen as carriers of the attributes of salvation, as well as with respect to the degree to which the major groups of the society were seen as having access to the major attributes of the cosmic and social order.

Closely related to differences between societies in their cultural orientations were differences in the organisational structures of their elites: the differentiation between different types of elites, in the scope of their internal autonomy, in their mutual access to one another, in the relative strength of secondary elites, and above all, in respect to the modes of control they exercised.

Such modes of control as exercised by different elites can be best distinguished according to the degree to which they entail or generate (a) different scopes (narrow or broad) of activity in major spheres and markets (economic, political, etc.) and especially the degree to which they cut across different ascriptive communities; (b) limitations in the flow of resources between such different markets and the convertibility of different resources, i.e., of economic into political ones or vice versa, as against their segregation; (c) the direction of flow of resources between different institutional markets i.e. the economic, political or prestige ones; (d) the breadth and diversity of the reference orientations that are constructed by the different elites.

Cultural orientations, structures of elites and modes of control in Europe

The particular interweaving of, structures of rulers and elites, the orientations they articulated and the modes of control they exercised in society were crucial variables in the patterning of different class structures and representation of interests. Let us therefore return to the European case and view the particular characteristics of elite groups there. From such a perspective we will be in a better position to view the dynamics underlying social stratification in different collectivities.

In Western and Central Europe there developed relatively multiple and autonomous elites with a high degree of specialisation between them and with a high degree of internal autonomy and autonomous access to the centre.[12] These elites carried multiple and cross-cutting orientations.[13] Most important among these orientations has been the emphasis on a high autonomy of the cosmic, cultural, and social orders and a high level of mutual relevance among them. This relevance was defined in terms of the tension between the transcendental and the mundane orders and in terms of the multiplicity and complexity of the different ways of resolving this tension, either through this-worldly (political and economic) or other-worldly activities, or usually through some combination of the two. The second cultural orientation prevalent in European civilisation has been a high level of activism and commitment of groups and strata and individuals to the cultural and social orders. Third has been the conception of a high degree of relatively autonomous access of different groups and strata to the centre—to some degree countered by, and in constant tension with the strong emphasis on the mediation of such access by such bodies as the Church or the political powers. Fourth, there developed in Europe a perception of a relatively close relation between the attributes of salvation and those of the basic primordial communities i.e., different regional collectivities were seen as carriers of such attributes.

In conjunction with their structure and orientations, the elites in Europe gave rise to relatively flexible class, ethnic, and political boundaries, to relatively broad multiple cross-cutting markets, multiple avenues of mutual conversion of different resources and broad access of many groups to such markets. Parallelly, these elites generated several specific tendencies of perception of the social field. Above all, they developed relatively broad, sometimes universalistic, diverse and mutually open definitions of criteria of membership of the basic societal collectivities (kinship, territorial, political, etc.), as well as of criteria of distributive justice (i.e., of the criteria according to which resources and positions are allocated).

These modes of control prevalent in European society gave rise to a very special type of pluralism. The type of pluralism Europe exhibited differed greatly from the one that can be found, for instance, in the compact Byzantine (or in the Russian) Empire, although this empire shared many elements of its cultural models with Western Europe. In the Byzantine Empire this pluralism was manifest in a relatively high degree of structural differentiation within a relatively unified sociopolitical framework in which different social functions were apportioned to different social categories. The structural pluralism that developed in Europe was characterised, above all, by a combination of steadily increasing levels of structural differentiation on the one hand, and constantly changing boundaries of collectivities, units and frameworks, on the other. This gave rise to several basic institutional characteristics: the most important of which were: (1) a multiplicity of centres even after the feudal period; (2) a high degree of permeation of the periphery by the centres and of impingement of the periphery on the centres; (3) a relatively small degree of overlapping of the boundaries of class, ethnic, religious and political collectivities and their continuous restructuring; (4) a comparatively high degree of autonomy of groups and strata and of their access to the centres of the society.[14]

Comparative notes on the structuring of social hierarchies

The preceding helps to identify certain broad patterns of interrelation between cultural orientations, the structures of elites, the modes of control they exercise and the way in which class interests, consciousness and activities are structured in Europe as compared to other societies.

The more autonomous elites articulating conceptions of a high degree of tension between transcendental and mundane orders, generate some general tendencies to relatively broad, sometimes universalistic, and diversified, definitions of criteria of membership of the basic societal collectivities (territorial, political, etc.), as well as of criteria of distributive justice (that is of the criteria according to which resources and positions are allocated and evaluated). Such autonomous elites tend also to encourage the development of relatively wide markets, as well as multiple avenues of conversion of different resources.

As against this, the less autonomous elites, developing in patrimonial or semi-patrimonial societies like those which can be found in parts of the Islamic world,[15] tend to generate narrower, more particularistic and less diversified definitions of the scope of membership of different communities and of distributive justice. They tend also to generate relatively narrower institutional markets, a low level of convertibility of different resources, and a low level of autonomous access to such markets.

Within the broad framework of the perception of tension between the transcendental and mundane orders several variations have been identified. Thus, the stronger the this-worldly emphasis carried by relatively monolithic elites, the higher will be the evaluation of political—cultural attributes and of the functional contribution to the maintenance of social order. The stronger the emphasis on 'other-worldly' orientations, the higher will be the evaluation of religious attributes and criteria, but these will tend to be dissociated from those of membership in primordial communities.

A continuous interweaving of this- and other-worldly conceptions of salvation carried by multiple autonomous elites, as was the case in Europe, seems to have reinforced the tendency toward a higher evaluation of multiple social and cultural attributes. As against this, a strong emphasis on segregation between this- and other-worldly conceptions of salvation (as was the case in Russia and to some degree in Byzantine and some Islamic societies) seems to have given rise to a high evaluation of functional contributions to the maintenance of social order and of political activities which are controlled by the political elites as against religious activities or of membership in basic primordial communities.[16]

The different definitions of scope of membership of the basic ascriptive communities and of criteria of distributive justice, related as they are to different world views and to different types of elites exercising different modes of control, also influence the structuring of the group bases of social hierarchies. In general, the tendency to structure 'class' interests in the direction of wide, up to country-wide, class consciousness is closely related to a relatively broad and diversified definition of criteria of membership and of distributive justice and hence to a strong emphasis on a perception of tension between the transcendental and the mundane orders.

Conversely, a relatively narrow definition of the criteria of membership—as developed by elites carrying a low perception of tension between the transcendental and the mundane order, or an otherworldly conception of resolution of such tension—tends to generate narrower and more variegated group bases of the structuring of social hierarchies. In such cases, these bases will be relatively narrow (family, neighbourhood, locality and ethnic) groups, the weaker will be the tendency toward the development of country-wide class consciousness based on general occupational or political religious criteria, and the stronger will be the tendency to cross-cutting vertical status arrangements.

The degree to which a specifically political articulation of class develops tends to depend upon the degree to which access to the major attributes of salvation and the social order are open to all members of the community. Conversely, if the degree of access of different groups to the centres of power is mediated by some monopolistic elites, the articulation of class will not develop as readily. Thus, the higher the degree of mediation, as has been the case in the Russian, Byzantine and Chinese Empires,[17] the smaller the possibility of such political expression of class interest and consciouness (except of those groups such as the Chinese *literati* in whom such mediation is vested). Alternatively, the weaker such emphasis on mediation, as was the case in Europe and to some degree in Islam, especially its Imperial polities, the more such access is open to all members of the community and the higher will be the tendency to some type of political consciouness.

The expression of class consciouness in political terms is greatly reinforced by situations in which the principle of autonomous access is posed against a *de facto* or mixed *de facto* and *de jure* monopolisation of such access by various upper groups, as was the case in most European early modern societies, and it is around the struggle to attain full control of the centre by the emerging, relatively new strata that the political articulation of class ideology tends to crystallise.

Insofar as such monopolisation of access to the centres is, as the case in the United Stated, nonexistent and the principles of political equality fully institutionalised in the centre, the tendency to such political expression of even wide class consciouness is very weak, as Werner Sombart has already noted at the beginning of this century.[18]

The preceding analysis indicates that, in broadest terms, there is a certain correlation between the structure of elites, the cultural orientations they carry, the modes of control they exercise and the structuring of social hierarchies and the modes of class-formation that develop in a society. Thus, the more autonomous elites tend to carry cultural orientations which entail a conception of tension between the transcendental and the mundane order, and which tend to develop relatively broad and flexible modes of control and accordingly relatively broader modes of group bases of social hierarchies as well as of articulation of class interest and consciouness.

Analytic conclusions and research perspectives

The preceding analysis has pointed out that among the various ideas it is—as has to a large degree been indicated, if not always systematically by Weber —the basic conceptions about the nature of the cosmic and social order and of their interrelations that are of great, importance in structuring the perception of different interests in general and class interests in particular. These ideas are important insofar as they become interwoven in the structure of power in general and of control over the flow of resources and over the perception of the social field by the major groups in particular, and in the struggles that develop around them. Furthermore the nature of such modes of control and the conflict they engender are greatly influenced by the contents of such ideas and by the closely related structure of their carriers.

These carriers are not, however, contrary to the suppositions of many theories of stratification, to be equated with the groups and strata which crystallise in a society as a result of the division of labour that develops within it. Rather it is the various elites analysed above and different coalitions of such elites, together with the representatives of such groups and strata, that are the crucial agents that exercise such modes of control.

Moreover the preceding analysis has indicated that the construction or institutionalisation of the major dimensions of social order is effected by: the specification of criteria of membership; of distributive justice and of access to power; by the construction of the symbolic maps of the social order; and by the concomitant modes of control over the production and flow of resources in any setting of social interaction. Each of these is effected by the special social actors analysed above.

Future research must thus be oriented towards (1) specifying the different aspects or modes of such control; (2) clarifying the symbolic definitions of the nature of the cosmic and social orders and their role in structuring the perception of different aspects of the social order by the members of a society within which they live; and (3) identifying specific social actors, and coalitions of elites who articulate such orientations and exercise these modes of control.

The following Chapters attempt to pursue research along these lines systematically and in the concrete settings of Southern Europe and the United States.

The arguments developed here are an elaboration of several themes first presented in 'Ideas and Interests: The Structuring of Social Hierarchies and Class Formations'. *Research in Social Stratification and Mobility*, **3** (1984): 209–36.

Notes

1. See G. E. Lenski, *Power and Privilege*, New York, McGraw Hill, 1966, pp. 10–12; R. Dahrendorf, *Class and Class Conflict in Industrial Society*, Stanford, Cal., Stanford University Press, 1964; C. Kerr, *Industrialism and Industrial Man*, Oxford, Oxford University Press, 1964; S. M. Lipset, 'Stratification, social class', pp. 296–316 in *International Enclyclopaedia of the Social Sciences*, Vol. 15. New York, Collier Macmillan, 1968; S. N. Eisenstadt, *Social Differentiation and Stratification*, Glenview, Scott, Foresman, 1971, Chaps. 7–10; and A. Giddens, *The Class Structure of the Advanced Societies*, London, Hutchinson University Library, 1973.

2. S. N. Eisenstadt, 'The Schools of Sociology', *American Behavioral Scientist* **24**, 1981, pp. 329–44.

3. S. M. Lipset, 'Social structure and social change', pp. 172–210 in P. Blau (ed.), *Approaches to the Study of Local Structure*, New York, Free Press, 1975, p. 172.

4. M. Weber, 'The Social Psychology of World Religions' in H. Gerth and C. W. Mills, *From Max Weber*, New York, Oxford University Press, 1946, pp. 267–301. On these controversies in the social sciences see; S. N. Eisenstadt, S. N. and M. Curelaru. *The Form of Sociology—Paradigms and Crises*, New York, Wiley, 1976.

5. See for instance, M. Bloch, *Feudal Society*, Chicago, University of Chicago Press, 1961; M. Beloff, *The Age of Absolution*, London, Hutchinson, 1954; P. Charanis, 'Internal strife at Byzantium in the Fourteenth Century', Byzantian **15**, 1940–41, pp. 208–30. 'The aristocracy of Byzantium in the thirteenth century', pp. 336–56 in P. R. Coleman, (ed.), *Studies in Roman Economic and Social History in Honor of A. C. Johnson*, Princeton, Princeton University Press, 1951.

6. M. S. Archer and S. Ginner, *Social Stratification in Modern and Contemporary Europe*, London, Weidenfeld and Nicholson, 1971.

7. See E. Balatz, *Chinese Civilization and Bureaucracy: Variations on a Theme* New Haven, Yale University Press, 1964; D. S. Nivison, And A. F. Wright, *Confucianism in Action*, Stanford, Stanford University Press, 1959; A. F. Wright, *Studies in Chinese Thought*, Chicago, University of Chicago

Press, 1953 and also *The Confucian Persuasion*, Stanford, Stanford University Press, 1960; and B. I. Schwartz, 'Transcendence in Ancient China', *Daedalus* **104**, 1975, pp. 57–68.

8. See for instance R. Pipes, *Russia under the Old Regime*, London, Weidenfeld and Nicholson, 1975; H. Seton-Watson, *The Decline of Imperial Russia 1855–1914*. London, Methuen, 1952; R. Feldmesser, 'Toward a classless society', pp. 522–33 in R. Bendix and S. M. Lipset (eds.), *Class, Status and Power*, New York, The Free Press, 1966; and A. Inkeles, 'Social stratification and mobility in the Soviet Union', pp. 516–62 in *ibid*.

9. On this topic in Islamic and Middle Eastern Societies see S. N. Eisenstadt, 'Convergence and Divergence in Modern and Modernizing Societies', *International Journal of Middle East Studies* **8**, 1970, pp. 1–27; J. A. Bill, 'Class Analysis and the Dialectics of Modernization in the Middle East', *International Journal of Middle East Studies* **3** 1972, pp. 417–34; and C. A. C. Van Nieuwenhuijze, *Social Stratification and the Middle East*, Leiden, E. J. Brill, 1965.

10. See Lenski, *Power and Privelege*.

11. M. Weber, *The Religion of China*, H. H. Gerth, (ed.), and trans. Glencoe, IL., Free Press, 1951; idem, *Ancient Judaism*, H. H. Gerth and D. Martindale, (eds.) and trans., New York, Free Press, 1952; and idem, *The Religion of India*, H. H. Gerth and D. Martindale, (eds.), and trans. Glencoe, IL., Free Press, 1952. On the Marxist position see A. Gramsci, *The Modern Prince and Other Writings*, London, Lawrence and Wishart, 1957.

12. S. I. Thrupp, *Early Medieval Society*, New York, Appleton-Century-Crofts, 1967; and F. Gilbert, (ed.), *The Historical Essays of Otto Hintze*, New York, Oxford University Press, 1975.

13. See J. J. O'Dea and C. Adams, *Religion and Man: Judaism, Christianity and Islam*, New York, Harper and Row, 1975; and E. Troeltsch, *The Social Teaching of the Christian Churches*, New York, Macmillan, 1931.

14. For greater historical detail see M. Bloch, 'Feudalism-European', pp. 203–10 in E. R. A. Seligman, (ed.), *Encyclopaedia of the Social Sciences* Vol. 6, New York, Macmillan, 1980; Block, *Feudal Society*; O. Brunner, *Neue Wege Der Sozialgeschichte*, Gottingen, Vandenhoeck and Ruprecht, 1966; and H. H. Cam, 'Mediaeval representation in theory and practice', *Speculum* **29**, 1957, pp. 347–55; J. Prawer and S. N. Eisenstadt, 'Feudalism, pp. 393–403 in D. L. Shils, (ed.), *International Encyclopedia of the Social Sciences*, New York, Macmillan, 1968.

15. S. N. Eisenstadt, *Traditional Patrimonialism and Modern Neo-Patrimonialism*, Beverly Hills and London, Sage Publications' Studies in Comparative Modernization Series, 1973.

16. For these perspectives on the social order see; E. Voegelin, *Order and History*, Vols. 1–3, Baton Rouge, Louisiana State University Press, 1954–56; E. Herr, 'The intellectual history of Europe', *The Beginnings of Western Thought to Luther*, Vol. 1. Garden City, NY, Anchor Doubleday, 1968; M. Raeff, *Origins of the Russian Intelligentsia: The Eighteenth Century*

Nobility, New York, Harcourt, Brace and World, 1966; G. E. Von Grunebaum, *Medieval Islam: A Study in Cultural Orientation*, Chicago, University of Chicago Press, 1946; H. G. S. Hodgson, 'The venue of Islam—conscience and history in a world civilization', *The Classical Age of Islam*, Vol. I., Chicago, University of Chicago Press, 1974; I. M. Lapidus, 'The separation of state and religion in the development of early Islamic society', *International Journal of Middle East Studies* **6**, 1975, pp. 363–85; J. M. Hussey, *Church and Learning in the Byzantine Empire* (867–1185), London, Oxford University Press, 1937.

17. On China see M. Freedman, *The Study of Chinese Society*, Stanford, Stanford University Press, 1979; and H. Fingarett, *The Secular as Sacred*, New York, Harper, 1972.

18. W. Sombart, *Why is There No Socialism in the United States?* C. T. Husbands (ed.), London, Macmillan, 1976.

7 Social stratification in Southern Europe

Luis Roniger

The singularity of Southern Europe

The Mediterranean areas of Southern Europe constitute a region whose singularity has been recurrently acknowledged both by those shaping national and international policies and by scholars in anthropology, sociology, and political science.

These areas have been, along with Ireland in Northern Europe, at the periphery of Western Europe since the seventeenth century, both economically and politically. Southern European societies have undergone wide transformations and modernised their political and economic structures since the early nineteenth century. Common lands were privatised, 'feudal' usages and paternalistic provisions were curtailed, and labour and land—'marketised'. Most of these areas have as well relatively long established traditions of incorporation into political entities and diversified social and economic structures. Compared with new nations in other continents, they cannot be considered 'underdeveloped' countries. Yet they share with 'underdeveloped' nations a singularity which has been maintained well into the twentieth century. For instance, compared to other countries in Western Europe these societies are only moderately industrialised and, to the present, a relatively high percentage of their economically active population has been engaged in agriculture and related activities (ranging in the late 1970s and early 1980s from 17 per cent of the economically active population in Italy and 20 per cent in Spain to 28 per cent in Greece and 32 per cent in Portugal). Although they had long been integrated within the capitalist world system and most have been or become members of the European Economic Community—with the inherent constraints on their economic functioning—their economic profiles still lag beyond other members of the organisation by most economic indicators such as internal composition by sectors, gross-national product per capita, or per capita energy consumption. Moreover, even where huge capital has been poured into regional economies such as the Italian South ($19,000 million in the period 1964–1975) dependence from metropolitan centres has remained prominent, migration of locals has continued, the wide use of State welfare payments has not diminished, and patronage politics has persisted as a salient feature as it was before. That is, throughout structural and other changes, continuities can be easily traced which have singled out Southern Europe as an area with specific problems and singular dynamics and dilemmas.[1]

In their social structure, they have shared with other modern societies basic trends of structural differentiation and stratification: a trend towards abolition or reduction of hereditary, legally upheld status differences; a high degree of structural and occupational differentiation; a shift of emphasis towards mobility and achieved rather than ascribed aspects of wealth and occupation; the weakening of legal and normative ascription; the breakdown of traditional closed relationships between property, power, and status; the widening of demands for social participation and for a more egalitarian distribution of resources in society.[2] Concomitantly, they have retained throughout modern times a number of idiosyncratic characteristics in their patterns of stratification. Among such characteristics the following stand out:

(a) strong inequalities in distribution and control of resources;
(b) complex strata categories and manifold (cross-cutting) layers of stratification;
(c) great value placed on prestige as a focus for evaluation of strata and conversion of resources;
(d) plurality of occupational commitments led by the same social actors;
(e) weakness of commitments to social class and other broad social categories;
(f) a tendency to narrow strata segregation both among upper and lower strata;
(g) conflicts both between strata and within strata.

This Chapter attemps to examine the extent to which these characteristics reflect the existence of a *sui generis* system of strata formation and interaction. Specifically, I shall inquire into the concomitant existence of strong actual and perceived inequalities in the distribution of resources, on the one hand, and the contest and cleavages emerging *within* social strata, on the other. In order to interpret this and other paradoxical combinations of features—which I shall describe in greater detail later on—social stratification will be analysed here from the perspective of the wider institutional, socio–cultural and political, matrices of these societies.

Internal differentiation and plurality of stratification schemes

Mediterranean European societies have been characterised by the per-sistance well into the nineteenth and twentieth centuries of a high variety of internal, regional differences in patterns of occupational differentiation and stratification. Thus, by the nineteenth century the following Spanish regions had full distinct social formations:

In the Vasque provinces of Guipúzcoa and Viscaya, scattered family holdings and non-partible inheritance patterns crystallised that led to the formation of an egalitarian ethos in a society cultivating intensive crops. In Alava and Southern Navarra, more aristocratic elements existed both in the villages and in urban ecclesiastic–administrative centres like Pamplona which contrasted with the more commercially oriented Bilbao and San Sebastián. In Asturias, the fertile coast contrasted with the poor soil of the hillside; complex tenancy and lease arrangements were maintained both by modest resident landlords and large absentee (but locally involved) landowners. The central Spanish plains were desolated and left to the great sheep pastoralists that had overwhelming influence and pasturage rights and which clashed with rural municipes living in hard conditions.[3] In Castilla, indebted tenants and peasants were involved in short term informal contracts, paying high rents to landlords. Even if there were some well-off peasants (around Salamanca and Valladolid, for instance), the majority struggled for a living. Rural landless workhands were numerous in Extremadura and Andalucía, which were regions of latifundia as well as of smallholdings on poor solid hilly areas). In Aragón transhumant large flocks were dominant, save for some dispersed settlement of poor agriculturalists. Minifundism characterised Galicia as well as populational pressure and migration especially after the liberal reforms of the 19th century which encroached on communal lands. Finally in Cataluña, the industrial–urban centres contrasted with both a declining traditional agricultural area and a prosperous wheat-and-diversified countryside.[4]

In Italy too a variety of stratification and land-tenure systems (and later industrial-urban systems) have been the rule.

In the late nineteenth century, the Alpine and hill areas of the North were dominated by small landownership. In Piedmont, Lombardy, Veneto and Liguria, small plots of infertile land were often held in scattered strips by peasants who combined work in them with seasonal migration to nearby cities or abroad and work in domestic industry, as well as with varied sharecropping arrangements. Subsistence farming predominated in the hill areas. Large landholding, wage labor, irrigation, and market-oriented specialised cropping characterized the fertile plains, in Lombardy for example. In Central Italy, *mezzadria* (sharecropping) arrangements were the rule. Latium was dominated by large (civil or ecclesiastic) landowners who leased lands to prosperous middlemen who, in turn, hired seasonal labor to farm fields. Southerners farmed land in the hillsides while large latifundia of absentee landlords were divided in varied types of subleasing arrangements. Landless labourers provided marginal workers and seasonal migrants. Within each of the above regions, differences existed such as those between East and West Sicily, and in addition microsocial situations added further sources of variation.[5]

Against such background of varied patterns of occupational differentiation, stratification schemes, and social formations it is little wonder that until recently few attempts have been made in the social sciences to analyse Southern European stratification structures in terms of *systems* of stratification.[6] Most social scientists have endorsed the view that it might be extremely 'abstract' and reductionist to talk of *a* Spanish or *an* Italian system of stratification, and more so of a Southern European system. Yet, many anthropological and socio-historical analyses of local and regional patterns of stratification have accumulated in the literature of the social sciences[7]; it may be instructive to look at what these works taken together, reveal about Southern European stratification as a whole. Accordingly, I shall try to discuss in a preliminary way the contradictory picture they posit with concern to this area.

Paradoxes in the study of stratification in Southern Europe

The anthropological and historical research conveys a picture of Southern European strata which is somehow contradictory. On the one hand, this literature emphasises the wide reliance of Southerners (Western Sicilians, Castillans, Greeks, etc.) on patron–client relations and patronage which are in a sense build on commitments that cut across the class structure and thus militate against class struggle.[8] On the other hand, a multitude of signs of class hostility are also described: peasant unrest, agrarian protest, anarchist and communist mobilisations. References abound as well to elites' hostility to lower classes, towards which they have shown disdain and avoidance for example, in statements along the lines of 'aquí no necesitamos hombres que piensen sino bueyes que trabajen'/not of thinking men we are in need but of working 'oxes'[9]).

Similarly, on a more political plane, references abound to a spirit of egalitarianism, sometimes embodied in common local residence, for instance in the Spanish *pueblo* which becomes a moral and not only a physical habitat, conveying 'a sense of compactness of groups of people drawn together and compressed into communities by external pressures common to both rural and urban situations'[10]; The *pueblo* comes to describe accordingly either a small town or village (and the sum of its inhabitants or rather of those committed to its spirit) or the Nation in its socio-moral character, that is, as opposed to other nations. Parallelly, analyses are found in the literature which emphasise structural dislocations and class struggle[11], as well as divisiveness reflected *within* political movements in the nineteenth and the twentieth centuries. Epitomes of such tendencies may be found in the post-war Italian Democratic Christian party, or the Spanish Democratic party of the 1860s.[12] The composition of the latter may be illustrative of such divisiveness: its ranks included radical progressives, monarchical democrats, unitarian republicans, federalist republicans, saintsimonians, fourerists, proudhonians, blanquists, cooperativists, plain socialists, republican socialists, krausists—all further separated by personal dissent and tensions. Thus, a contradictory picture is conveyed in the literature of Southern European societies being characterised by both unity and divisiveness, by both hierarchical inter-class commitments and class hostility and struggle.[13]

Traditionally, psychological arguments were advanced for explaining the subsequent cycles of revolutionary upheaval and melancholic quietism. For Andalucía, for example, these cycles were traced back by authors such as Díaz del Moral or Raymond Carr to the persistence of an atavistic Arab character there.[14] Parallel explanations have been attempted by scholars interested in 'false consciousness'. Such scholars have attempted to isolate the structural conditions which could render such ideological constructs as 'amoral familism' or patronage to be epitomes of false consciousness.[15] Concomitantly, it has been argued that patronage systems exacerbate rather than mitigate class struggle, implying this might explain the pattern of intermitent but harsh class struggle in Southern Spain.[16] Drawing mostly on data from the South Asian subcontinent, Hamza Alavi suggested once that there are problems of mediation of class struggle by primordial loyalties[17]; this claim seems connected with Sydel Silverman's Italian findings on the crucial importance of the domestic cycle as articulating economic activities and thus allowing or hampering changes in Mediterranean value systems.[18] Such lines of research, suggestive as they are, emphasise—sometimes, in contradiction to the manifested assumptions and proclaimed aims of the researchers—that issues such as the structuring of social hierarchies and political struggles are intimately interwoven with broader value assumptions and cultural orientations.[19]

Thus, in order to make the alluded contradictory traits intelligible, the necessity arises of focusing attention on the connections between value orientations and structural conditions in the shaping of social hierarchies in Southern Europe. To begin this endeavour, I shall discuss hereafter what seem to be the basic characteristics of social stratification in Central and Southern Spain (as represented by Castille, Andalucía and to a lesser extent, Aragón) and in Southern Italy (especially in the continental Mezzogiorno and in Western Sicily). These have been the main areas within Spain and Italy where the above noted traits have been most felt, at least as reflected in the literature of the social sciences.[20]

Basic characteristics of Spanish and Italian social stratification

The social settings under consideration have had highly differentiated systems of stratification characterised by strong unequal distribution of material resources; a little overlapping of class, ethnic, religious, and political lines of affiliation and commitment; and a tendency towards hierarchisation of socio-economic and political life. Even where small peasant villages were relatively homogeneous in their class composition and life styles, they were still segmented in a highly hierarchised structure of economic exchange and of politico-administrative control by the State and its machinery.[21]

Accordingly, high differentiation and hierarchisation have been typical of both national class structures. Focusing on post-war Italy, we find that descriptions abound in the literature based on the existence of a plurality of 'classes'.[22] Thus;

(a) landed propertied classes, holding property rights but estranged from agricultural labour, seldom involved in the management of holdings, usually, receiving rents from tenants; in the North, bourgeois orientations, engagement in capitalistic farming through the employment of propertyless rural workers, and prestige granted to 'modern' rather than 'traditional' landed proprietors; in the South, more paternalistic (patronage) oriented landowners, involved in agriculture under a situation of non-competitiveness of production costs;
(b) independent entrepreneurs, employing up to 80 per cent of the total industrial labour force, once politically powerful and prestigeous (in the period 1870–1910, when state policies and bills favoured them), their

position was reduced in the late twentieth century *vis-à-vis* corporations and trade unions as well as compared with that of business managers, professionals and career politicians; their wealth, reduced by the comparative lower productivity of their firms;

(c) a large service class, providing highly skilled services such as legal, administrative, financial, insurance and medical services;

(d) managers of big industry (e.g. steel or chemicals) which developed since the late nineteenth century with the aid of state protective tariffs and under conditions of war production demands and favourable labour conditions; after the 1930s and second war crises, a group of young managers, with wide personal and business networks throughout Europe and a dominant class position within Italy;

(e) professional politicians, since the postwar period, a mildly conservative political group with middle or lower service class or intellectual backgrounds; comprising the higher regional and national officials of the political parties and their representatives and senators; ranking low in wealth and prestige, have cornered high political power partly due to the state control over nationalised industries, the need for state investment and protectionist industrial policies in face of international competition, monetary crises, and political unrest;

(f) state bureaucrats, a very large group, tracing their origins to the Piedmontese civil service, with relative high degree of job security and de facto control over administrative implementation of policies;

(g) industrial workers, unorganised, fragmented, and high exploited in Southern Italy and the islands; in the modern sectors, large numbers organised sectorially and corporately; there has been a contemporary decrease in internal differentiation in this class;

(h) rural workers—extremely differentiated internally.

As we move closer to regional and local levels, such a picture of minute class differentiation and hierarchisation is replicated to an even greater detail, at least for those strata segments that comprise the local social hierarchies. For instance, retaining focus on Italy, the Western Sicilian stratification system comprised the following sectors in the period of Italian unification[23]:

(a) an aristocracy (the *nobili*) living in Palermo, in mainland Italy or abroad;

(b) the clergy, connected by kinship with the class of small leaseholders and small landowners (*burgisi, contadini agiati*);

(c) a wide stratum of big leaseholders, above all the so-called *gabelotti*, i.e. large scale tenants paying tenancy in money and the *massari*, i.e.

rich peasants who did not subdivide land but worked it themselves with servants and hired labour, chiefly, cattle breeders. Upper levels formed by *civili*, *borghesi*, and *professionisti*, i.e. landholders who did not work but followed a profession such as law, medicine, pharmacy, or were merchants and teachers;

(d) artisans (*maestri*, *artigiani*);
(e) small sharecroppers (*mezzadri*);
(f) landless peasants (*braccianti*, *solariati*, *giornalieri*); and
(g) at the lowest level of the scale, goatherds and shepherds (*caprai* and *pecorai*).

Thus, strong inequalities have characterised the structure of stratification in the area. It follows that social classes may be classified—as researchers following the so-called 'nominalist' school in stratification studies have done—in terms of criteria deemed objective, such as wealth or control of material resources.[24] A more critical perspective is provided, however, by analysing the value people themselves have placed on such schemes of stratification, that is, by the reflection of social inequalities on the perception of social actors. We may look once more at the scheme of strata classification brought hereabove and describe the way local people conceptualised it. According to H. Hess, Western Sicilians thought of the above noted classification in terms of a threefold system of (a) *nobili*; (b) *cappeddi* or *gente de paese*, i.e. urbanities, comprising the 'middle classes'; and (c) *biritti* or *gente di campagna*, i.e. rural folks, comprising the 'lower classes'.[25] Such a classificatory scheme was guided by the perceived relative closeness or distance of strata to an urban *style* of life and behaviour. That is, not merely by a claimed urban residence but rather by the attribution of an urbanised style of life.

The reliance on behavioural styles is due to two parallel ecological and social processes that have taken place in Western Sicilian society. First, the fact that Southern Italian patterns of settlement have been until recently one of general village residence, in the so-called agro–towns, rather than one of isolated and dispersed settlement in farms.[26] Due to such varied factors as fragmented land ownership and leases, subsistence agriculture, unhealthy lowlands, and especially a long tradition of internecine warfare, banditry and recurring invasions, most peasants have settled in the agro–towns which were a kind of 'dormitories' for the nearby latifundia and peasant plots. While it cannot be denied that an 'urbanised' style of life has been highly praised, lines of urban–rural distinction and residence have been at most blurred and no dichotomous residence patterns crystallised during the nineteenth and twentieth centuries.[27] Second, naturally enough for an agrarian society, the evaluative criteria of social actors revolved around the value placed on land.[28] However, this evaluation was not free of contradictions. Thus, on the one hand, land was a basic means of livelihood and security, and its possession granted respectability, i.e. was a means for attaining high status. As such, land was for decades a major focus of conversion of resources on the part of sectors with acquisition power such as merchants, bureaucrats, and entrepreneurs. Southern middle and professional classes sought to acquire land and thereafter acted as absentee landowners rather than as rural entrepreneurs.[29] But, on the other hand, a too close relation to the land was a hindrance to high status, due to the need to engage in manual labour which was viewed as defiling in Italy as much as in Spain.[30] Thus, it seems that while the major criteria for evaluating strata have been connected with power and wealth, these have been praised not only in themselves, but mainly as means for attaining a 'clean' (nonmanual) and a 'civilised' (urbanised) style of life which was considered to be honourable and prestigious.

To put the above in more general terms, high value has been placed traditionally on prestige and proofs—or, at least, indications—of a civilised 'quality' as a major dimension for evaluating strata and individuals in Southern European stratification systems. In the pre-modern periods of these societies, this tendency was mainly focused, as already indicated, on land or alternatively on an entrepreneurial (including a *mafioso*) style of forceful advancement of interests by individuals of a lower-middle class agrarian origin. In the modern period and in modern sectors, foci changed of course; for instance, journalism became in postwar Italy a major focus of identity for elitist-status seeking politicians.[31] Notwithstanding such changes in foci, a prestigious way of life still remained at the apex of the criteria for strata evaluation.

Several additional features are connected with and in fact mediate this dominant trend. First, as economic wealth and power do not automatically confer social standing, differences in the control of resources do not necessarily convey hierarchial class distinctions. This differential control of resources must be channelled ('converted') into ranking precedence in terms of behavioural styles. Beyond ideological constructs, this implies that many dimensions of social life, such as encounters at the market place or municipal affairs, are not closed to individuals of the lower strata but rather have been defined as open, despite sharp inequalities in wealth and power, and have been conceived to be regulated by what Julian Pitt-Rivers has called the rule of 'first come, first served'.[32]

Second, claims for ranking precedence, which are supported by differences in wealth and power, have been phrased in terms of honour. That is, in terms which ultimately can be referred to moral grounds (even to 'human traits' such as the virility of men and the 'pure' or 'impure' behaviour of women) and as such may be subject to contest across the scale of stratification. Under such circumstances, disputes may arise around claims for equality or deferent relations made by members of the lower and upper classes segments, respectively.[33]

Third, the above disputes may be dealt by protocol regulation, by personal arrangements that may cut across any 'objective' ranking lines, by forceful means, etc. What is fundamental here is that whatever the means employed, no normative regulation is provided to guarantee that disputes should be avoided or settled prescriptively.

Fourth, typical of such situations is the fact that moral implications are attributed to the different actions employed by social actors, including the use of physical violence.[34]

Fifth, and of foremost importance for the structuring of social hierarchies, was the embodiment of behavioural styles in prestigious symbols related to central dimensions of social order: literacy, piety, nobility of character and way of life, concern for the public good, and so on. Accordingly, social strata have tended to segregate themselves from similar occupational and social groups either from other regions or from one another in the same region. Hence, a tendency has emerged in this area whereby the boundaries of significant social groups tended to be defined in the relatively narrow terms of their own symbols of prestige and claims to social precedence.[35]

Thus far, several traits of Southern European stratification systems have been indicated: the centrality of behavioural styles and prestige as criteria for structuring social hierarchies; the openness of markets and potential contest across the scale of stratification; the lack of normative regulation to guarantee that disputes should be avoided or settled prescriptively; and the tendency of strata to segregate themselves from similar occupational or social groups.

Political implications

The political consequences of these patterns of stratification are of a contradictory nature. Class grievances and movements of protest in this area have often coalesced or even become identified with political dissent, involving an intensive rhetoric of collective orientations and visions of comprehensive social reorganisation; as such, they have met with repression and the exclusionary policies by the political centres and central elites of society. An illustration of this trend may be seen in the convergence and coalescence in Italy during the 1860s and 1870s of the *brigantaggio* raids in the South, the local opposition to a milling tax (the *maccinato*), and the resistence to the efforts of the new political regime to administer the territories under its aegis; these were in addition paralleled by the antigovernmental demonstrations led by political opponents of the Italian state-holders who expressed their allegiance to the old regimes or, as in the case of the Republicans in the 1870s, tried to bring about more radical policies. Similarly, the food riots, agricultural strikes, tax protests, and organised land seizures of the 1880s and 1890s, became connected with the formation of political labour organisations such as the *Partito Operaio* that inspired mobilisations of *braccianti*, and with the expansion of franchise and the electoral success of Socialists who introduced the first laws regulating employment and working conditions. At that time, the reformist demands of workers such as those of the capitalist agrarian Po Valley were met by a strong repression on the part of the owners and the State, which led to radicalisation of demands and ideologisation of protest which was directed and oriented towards the broader socio-political order of Italian society. From these and many other movements of protest a picture emerges of wide collective mobilisations.[36]

At the same time, however, Southern European stratification systems have been characterised by an opposite trend: the plurality of occupational identities and commitments pursued by individuals both within the upper and lower strata, which weakens categorical broad commitments. For instance, a variety of occupational roles have been followed by members of the lower strata either simultaneously or in rapid succession: working on one's scattered strips of land has been combined with the lease of plots, the arrangement of sharecropping agreements, seasonal migration, hired farm labour, etc. Such patterns of multiple job holding created situations of intermingling of roles and fragmentation of occupational identities hampering the formation of broad categorical commitments among wide strata groupings such as the peasantry and working classes.

The tendency towards fragmentation of categorical (class) identities has been particularly exacerbated where it was reinforced by non-integration or instability of means of livelihood, fragmentation of economic activities, ecological isolation and fluctuating economic resources. Fragmentation has however also been found in the urban centres and among the upper strata not suffering economic deprivation. The fragmentation of occupational identities and class commitments has persisted too, into modern times in so far as new occupational roles have been merely added to traditional ones instead of creating new mechanisms for relating economic activities into the normal processes of daily routine and domestic cycle.

In sum we can say that the characteristics of Southern European class politics were related to the paradoxical combination of strong inequalities in wealth, along with great value placed on prestige rather than on control of material resources as a focus for evaluation of strata and for conversion of resources; and by trends towards strata segregation and fragmentation of status categories, along with a plurality of occupational identities held by social actors and hence by weakness of categorical commitments. In other words, by a tendency towards sharp consciousness of strata differentials, yet not by the structuring of such differentials into clear-cut strata and, hence, by wide room left to individual efforts, manipulations of contacts and mobility channels in attaining specific placement in the stratification scheme. The nature of foci for such efforts and struggles—around issues of honour, personal dignity, precedence in ritual and non-ritual occasions, etc.—indicate that a tension is found in such societies between the moral and ideological dimensions of social life which predicate openness of goods for all social actors, irrespective of differences in wealth and power, and the more hierarchical facets of construction of social hierarchies which are predicated upon the unequal distribution of material, economic and political, resources.

These tendencies have been fundamental in effecting the crystallisation of images of villagers' unity and cooperation at the local level, but also of strong internal competition and conflict in rural and urban settings. That is, competition has not been restricted to class opposition but has been found as well among 'equals' traditionally engaged in antagonistic contests for greater shares of resources and for honour and family reputation.[37]

Stratification studies and the study of Southern European stratification

Throughout the preceding analysis, the major traits of Southern European social hierarchies have been outlined. Are these characteristics congruent with the assumptions of previous Western approaches to stratification? These approaches, as described and criticised by S. N. Eisenstadt[38] have assumed that social hierarchies are shaped by the level of development of technology and structural differentiation; that only (economic and political) power elements are central in structuring social hierarchies and class formations; that such structuring is correlated specifically to marketisation and capitalistic transformation of modern economies and to political modernisation; that it is crystallised in the form of rather coherent classes with a high degree of status association, autonomous access (or denial of access) to power, country-wide strata or class consciousness (and hence, even if only implicitly acknowledged, a low impingement of ethnic, religious and regional cleavages); and, finally, a high degree of political articulation and expression of class interests and conflicts.

The discussion thus far has indicated—even if only along broad lines—several qualifications to the above, when approached from a Mediterranean perspective.

First, the discussion has confirmed that structural (occupational and technological) differentiation has far-reaching influence in the structuring of social hierarchies in the region but, parallelly, has indicated that a high degree of strata differentiation was also typical of traditional settings and not only of modern ones.

Second, that differences in wealth and power were fundamental in such processes of stratification but that status and prestige played a no less important role both as major criteria for evaluation as well as foci for conversion of resources in traditional as well as in modern settings.

Third, the above analysis has indicated that the characterisation of strata as broad associations was not reflected in the ways people perceived social strata. Indeed, people held narrower conceptions that generated segregation, internal cleavages and contest, an overlapping of class identities, and a weakness of categorical commitments. Yet, at various periods (in fact more in Spain than in Italy) strong conflicts exploded which combined class grievances with political dissent and involved large mobilisations of population, thus indicating a basic trend toward broader and active participation in the political centre and attempts to open access to *loci* of power in society.

The above qualifications, as well as the more detailed analysis of characteristics of stratification in the area, indicate that the configuration of social hierarchies has been intimately connected with the significance and broader meanings that social actors—individuals and strata alike—have attributed to the regulation of resources, wealth and power in these societies, as well as those concerning the place of trust and solidarity or of distrust and struggle in collective life. It is within such a framework of interweaving of cultural orientations and structural factors that the seemingly contradictory traits enumerated at the beginning of this paper become more meaningful. Accordingly, it is to a discussion of the impact of such orientations in the structuring of social hierarchies in this area, that we turn in the following section.

Basic orientations and the structuring of social hierarchies in Southern Europe

From a comparative perspective, European civilisations in general and Western European societies in particular have been characterised by a symbolic pluralism and a multiplicity of cultural orientations being reflected in several institutional characteristics: the formation of multiple centres; the high degree of permeation and mutual impingement and centres and peripheries; a comparatively high degree of autonomy of groups and strata and of their access to the centres of society; relatively high levels of political activity; a multiplicity of cultural, professional, economic elites, cross-cutting each other and closely connected to broader strata; the relative autonomy of the legal systems with regard to the political and religious realms; the emergence of cities as autonomous centres of social and cultural creativity and sources of identification and identity; and the continuous restructuring of class, ethnic, religious, communal and political boundaries.[39]

Such multiplicity implies that a weak institutional connection has existed between the cultural, universalistic orientations of these societies and the actual social and political order. In a parallel manner, it implies that competing visions would be advanced by various social forces oriented to 'close' the perceived gap between natural order and law and actual institutional arrangements. Such competing visions, articulated by various centres and elites, clashed with each other particularly due to the framework of internal social differentiation and ecological cleavages, but were projected also to the modern, and more 'unified', period of these societies.

The above implies as well—as discussed in greater detail in Chapter three in this book—that political struggle as well as advancement of social demands revolved not only around technical aspects and procedural matters but addressed at the same time basic issues such as the common identity of different social groups with its correlated implications. First, the establishment of institutional credit and access to power and resources to be granted to different social groups or gained by them. Secondly, the settlement of 'prices' and conditions for the entitlement of access to public goods, the public distribution of private goods, etc. Connected to the former, struggles addressed as well the question of the degree of legitimacy granted to the political system in connection with the character of access or exclusion of different social and political forces to/from the *foci* of public authority, and in connection with the specific institutional channels whereby disagreements on these issues would be settled.

Within such framework, a basic indeterminacy has crystallised in the structuring of social hierarchies. This indeterminacy, further emphasised by the overlapping of class, ethnic, religious, and political identities in Southern Europe, increases in turn the significance for social actors of turning market situations to their advantage; foremost, in what concerns control of resources and avenues for the conversion of resources.

Thus, on the one hand, powerful elements may entrench themselves at the apex of the local and regional social structures, exploiting and despising those engaged in manual labour; these elements may try to monopolise positions of control of resources as soon as there is a relatively organisationally strong administrative centre willing to back them or as soon as conditions are found locally for such endeavour (for instance where prospects of migration for better salaries and employment are slim).

On the other hand, such situations of indeterminacy do not assure that these social forces would attain a legitimate claim to wealth and power which might be anchored in the broader meanings sustained in these societies. Accordingly, prestigious positions and high status become, as has been shown above, a major dimension for validating or denying recognition to positions of wealth and power. The focus on status projection and honour leaves contest for respectability in a sense open to all social strata, since it is anchored (besides in power and wealth) in moral grounds. In a sense, of course, a powerful position may place its bearer beyond the effective blow of moral attacks but nonetheless the structuring of social hierarchies is left open to the impact of opposed claims and visions held by different social groups, strata segments and individuals.

Thus, the cultural matrix of these societies seem to have conditioned the expression of social demands and protest in highly ideological and collective terms. Though these coalesced and were perceived *in political terms*, at the same time, a basic indeterminacy existed in the structuring of social hierarchies. This indeterminacy has left room first, for contrasting visions on the proper structuring of the socio-political order; and, second, for the emergence of strong hierarchical trends of control of resources that lack normative sanction.

As a result of these somehow opposed tendencies, a pattern has emerged—especially among incumbents to the political centre and elites, but also among other strata—of potential competition around positions of power and control of resources and avenues for the conversion of resources. Struggles are not confined to 'opposed' classes but come to characterise as well interaction between members of the same social categories, thus creating instability, continuous contest, manipulation and perpetual imbalances. Under certain conditions, these instabilities compel social actors to conduct their contest for valued resources through parallel clusters of patron–client, unwritten agreements between partners commanding unequal resources and belonging to different social categories. Such agreements and relations have been widely used by Southern Europeans depending upon factors such as the existence or lack of electoral politics or the ratio of available work opportunities to labour forces.[40]

The weakness of categorical commitments and inner divisiveness of strata has been also found within coalitions involved in situations of political confrontations with other forces, where supposedly 'broader' demands and class protest and conflicts were at the stake, as occurred in the Andalucian countryside in the late nineteenth and early twentieth centuries.

A second aspect of the above indeterminacy concerns the forms of access to power attained by social strata. Situations have been discussed above of a low categorical (intra-strata) commitment. Yet, a major aspect of political mobilisation in the societies under consideration has been the intense ideological rhetoric of collective (including class) conflict which has projected alternative visions for a future reorganisation of the basic tenets of society and which has combined worldly struggles and other-worldly orientations, and a collective outlook towards an active participation in the shaping of the social and political order.

That is, especially in so far as new social strata demanded the extension of rights hitherto denied them, struggles have been initiated by social groups and networks conceiving society in terms of a closed class system, in terms of suposedly existent 'limited Good' (the term is Foster's[41]) being placed under harsh contest by opposed social forces as well as by members of the same strata; and, until modern times, in terms of relatively minor possibilities of social mobility. Parallely, in those struggles instrumental interests have been advanced in the form of universalistic demands and broad collective (e.g. class) symbols. Accordingly, such struggles have projected ultimate and collective claims which often have been rejected and were not accommodated, as shown in the period that preceded the Spanish civil war. In other instances, they led to a corporatist incorporation of demands, as shown in the case of the Italian Sicilian *Fasci* of the late nineteenth century and the Communist party in the postwar period.

The rejection of protest demands was further related to class symbols considered by opposed social forces to be in contradiction with national interests and, as such, to be fought as alien to the core values of society. The fact remained nevertheless that the contesting ideologies were phrased in reference to the same core of ultimate values which shaped the civilisational discourse and contours of the socio-political order. Moreover, social movements, which maintained variants of 'totalistic' orientations and ideologies struggled with each other forcefully, as illustrated in the case of Spanish socialists, anarchists, and anarcho-syndicalists.[42]

Articulation of demands and incorporation of protest

The above analysis indicates that social demands and protest have tended, beyond the interpersonal and more individualistic levels, to become expressed periodically in high ideological terms and to be perceived in political terms. Against the background of indeterminacy of social hierarchies, discussed in the preceding sections, the impact of strata demands and social grievances has been mediated by the specific form of centre–periphery relations and the conceptions and projects which, around the structuring of the socio-political order, have been carried by elites both in Spain and Italy. It is therefore necessary to analyse, albeit in a preliminary way, how social demands and protest have impinged and been incorporated or rejected within such institutional frameworks.

Southern European societies have presented in the modern period a combination of processes of wide activism and subsequent demobilisation and mediation in access to *loci* of power. In principle, access to the latter was assumed to be mediated by social actors that articulated social models of order and which were in part embodied in the central elites. In fact, there have been sporadic and recurrent explosions of activism in in local communities and among occupational and status groups. Such epitomes of activism were found, for instance, during periods of weakened central rule and wide popular mobilisation (as during the so-called Spanish War of Independence in 1808–1814, when the traditions of autonomous municipal affairs and delegation of power which characterised the Medieval Cortes, gained new strength). But these phases of wide mobilisation were soon 'tamed' during subsequent periods of peace, by exclusivist drives on the part of elites which came to mediate the socio-political participation of broader strata. This mediation was effected in both countries first through the development of clientelistic articulation of demands by patrons with local power domains or by other social actors connected to the centres of power and acting as brokers between the latter and the population. Second, through the inclusion of 'natural' social groups, or those constituted artificially by the centre, within a corporativist frame of representation and cooptation. Clientelistic networks and corporatist frameworks have been major institutional mechanisms used for the concomitant control of social groups and the building of loyalties—useful in advancing individual or sectoral interests and in securing access to sought goods and services.

These forms of articulation of demands and expression of protest have undergone many transformations in their concrete unfolding which cannot be elaborated further here for reasons of space. Nonetheless, beyond variations and changes, it is possible to single out several features, listed below, that have have been particularly salient in connection with articulation of social demands and impingement of protest in the Southern European polities.

First, the restrictive character of political participation granted to social forces by the central elites stood in contrast to the perception of such participation, ideally conceived as open to all members of the collectivity.

Second, the central political forces were found to be prone to be responsive to demands of social strata mainly in particularised (individualised and, later, collective) clientelistic terms.

Third and connected to the foregoing, collective movements of protest have met often exclusive policies of repression on the part of central political forces who, besides rejecting specific demands, have denied them recognition. Many of these movements have accordingly exacerbated the totalistic character of their ideological tenets and have conceived themselves and were perceived to be a potential or actual alternative to the given social order. Struggles, even if economic and stemming from specific demands, have tended to become rapidly oriented to the political realm and to be articulated as against the symbols of the centre and its structures.

Fourth, the configuration of the political realm has often been considered to be solely the result of the constellation of forces at any given time and, as such, was considered a focus for continuous struggle—potentially shattering in its effects. The low degree of mutual commitment of the various clientelistic clusters that composed the government structures reinforced such potentiality.

Fifth, and related to the preceding feature, social and regional plurality have been seen as endangering collective identity. Such an identity has been often conceived in holistic terms of unity and centralisation and has been predicated towards the suppression of peculiarities rather than to their connection to the collective identity.

Sixth, the centres closed themselves thereby to the demands and tensions found in the social structure and failed to build institutionalised channels of access to *loci* of power and decision-making. In turn, the regulative policies of such centres could therefore have been seen as 'predatory' and 'alien', with two interconnected consequences. On the one hand, social forces sought to obstruct them, bringing the structural weaknesses of specific regimes and coalitions to the fore. On the other hand, articulation of demands often assumed an extra-parliamentary focus, reinforcing thereby the reformulation of a schism between the formal principles and the informal (but 'real') workings of the political system.

Seventh, struggles over social equality and political rights, have often been conceived as related to attempts to change the contours of the collective identity. In this connection, changes of policy have been interpreted as expressions of partisan interests—both by beneficiaries and those excluded from benefits.

Naturally enough, as in any other society, movements of protest were effective to various degrees when oriented to a specific re-structuring of distributive justice in the social system. But these movements, pervasive and violent as they were in Spain and Italy, elicited responses that only occasionally enhanced the flexibility of the political systems to deal with some of the main issues that these modern nation–states faced such as the specification of rules of distributive justice in connection with the definition of the exact contents of the collective identity and the question of legitimacy. When protest was perceived to be concerned with such issues, it was met not through the institutionalisation of workable arrangements connecting social forces to the political centre in an enduring manner, but through repression, or co-optation. Consequently movements of protest and opposition succeeded in changing such ground rules of definition of social hierarchies only through force, as shown in the case of the Italian fascists and the Franquist forces in Spain.

The Italian and Spanish cases were however marked by major differences in the articulation and incorporation of protest demands. Differences connected in part with the major orientations and policies of the political centres and in part derived from their differential administrative capacity. Thus, while both the Spanish and the Italian political centres have been characterised by extractive policies of incorporation of peripheries along with an organisational incapacity to implement such incorporation, variations existed between the administrative capability of these centres to realise such drives, with Spain having a greater capacity than Italy to penetrate the least mobilised areas of agrarian capitalism (parts of Andalucia and Extremadura in Spain, Western Sicily in Italy). The Spanish political centre was also more motivated in such extractive policies than the Italian, due to its conception of imperial historical tradition and, of no less significance, due to its location in a region of non-economic significance and its financial weakness. By contrast, the ruling elites in Italy had to work out (from the 1860s onwards) the bases of legitimacy of the new state and therefore were driven to use cooptation to broaden their bases of support; in a relatively short period, enfranchisement was granted to wide sectors and mass parties appeared in electoral contests.[43]

Within such context, it was Spain—where social and political cleavages acquired territorial connotations and the centre was extractive in extreme— that workable regimes fully endorsed policies of centralisation as shown by such ideologically distinct regimes as the Franquist, and the Democratic of the early 1980s; it was also there that social protest and conflict, while being oriented to the centre, adopted extreme and often tragic connotations. By contrast, in Italy national participation originated in the economically advanced areas of the North, conflicts were found almost on a village-to-village level, embracing forces identified with political actors confronting each other on the national level, and major social actors adopted more pragmatic forms of mutual accomodation, remaining committed in the long term to participation in the political centre.

From all these vantage points, and beyond the specificities of each case, it seems that while collective social protest has been oriented to the political realm and has tended to coalesce and be considered identical with political demands and struggle, it was met by policies of demobilisation of social forces, centralisation of decisions, and mediated access to *loci* of power. I would like to suggest that this has probably reinforced the perception of the socio-political order as an arena for confrontations as well as the denial of broader commitment to actual political arrangements, save when they favour partisan interests. This may have reinforced in turn the tendencies to status segregation, low degree of categorical commitments, the wide use of patron–client relations and, indirectly, hindered the structuring of clear-cut strata. formation, despite the sharp consciousness of strata differentials typical of both traditional and modern Southern European societies.

Conclusion

This Chapter has identified the existence of a basic indeterminacy in the structuring of Southern European, specifically Spanish and Italian, modern systems of stratification. This indeterminacy, which partakes of the historical experience of Western European settings, implies that the formation of highly differentiated social hierarchies and a sharp consciousness of strata differentials have not been obliterated in the area. It implies nonetheless that these ideological (hierarchical) conceptions could not assure that social strata would attain legitimation and recognition of claims to wealth, to social standing and to political power in a prescriptive way. Wide room has been left to individual initiative and collective efforts in attaining specific placement in the scales of stratification. In this context, two contrasting tendencies have been dominant in the advancement of social demands and political participation. On the one hand, intermittent class struggle and ideological rhetoric have been pursued against the perceived closed aspects of the system of hierarchies, being phrased along universalistic and collective motives and themes. But, in parallel manner these societies have been characterised as well by particularistic patronage arrangements, ego-centred networks struggling for a greater share of resources, and intra-class cleavages and contest within the various social strata, as well as by trends towards strata segregation along narrow lines, restricted political participation, and social control through mediation and through corporatist frameworks of articulation. It is within the analytical framework followed here that what seemed to be contradictory trends can better be comprehended as part of the same dynamics; a dynamics in which the value orientations of social actors appear to be as crucial as economic differentiation in shaping the contours of social hierarchies and the patterns of strata participation in Southern European societies.

Notes

1. This specificity has been recognised in the use of labels such as 'Mediterranean' which have been widely applied to Southern European societies. For some of the socio-economic indicators referred to above see the chapter on 'Western Europe' in W. J. Feld and G. Boyd, (eds.), *Comparative Regional Systems*, New York, Pergamon Press, 1980. See also T. B. Bottomore, 'Class Structure in Western Europe', pp. 388–406 in H. G. Archer and S. Giner, (eds.), *Contemporary Europe*, London, Weidenfeld and Nicholson, 1971.

2. On these trends see S. N. Eisenstadt, *Social Differentiation and Stratification*, chapter 7, Glenview, Scott, Foreman and Co., 1971.
3. The classic work on the great sheep pastoralists and their impact on the economic and social structure of Spain is J. Klein, *The Mesta*, Port Wahington, Kennikat Press, 1964.
4. On the regional diversity of nineteenth century Spain see among others R. Carr, *España, 1808–1936*, chapter 1, Barcelona, Ariel, 1978.
5. M. Clark, *Modern Italy, 1871–1982*, London and New York, Longman, 1984.
6. For pioneer although uneven works see R. T. Anderson, *Modern Europe: An Anthropological Perspective*, Pacific Palisades, Goodyear Publishing Co., 1973; and J. Davis, *People of the Mediterranean*, London, Routledge and Kegan Paul, 1976.
7. The Northern Mediterranean has been one of the earliest *loci* of anthropological research. See for instance C. Gower Chapman, *Milocca: A Sicilian Village*, New York, Shenkman, 1971 (originally published in 1928).
8. See for instance A. Blok, 'Mafia and Peasant Rebellion as Contrasting Factors in Sicilian Latifundism', *Archives Européennes de Sociologie*, **10**, 1969, pp. 95–116; and A. H. Galt, 'Rethinking Patron-Client Relationships: The Real System and the Official System in Southern Italy', *Anthropological Quarterly*, **47**, 1974, pp. 182–202.
9. J. Díaz del Moral, *Historia de las agitaciones campesinas andaluzas*, p. 74 note 5, Madrid, Alianza, 1979.
10. M. Kenny, 'Parallel Power Structures in Catile: The Patron-Client Balance', p. 156 in J. G. Peristiany, (ed.), *Contributions to Mediterranean Sociology*, Paris-The Hague, Mouton, 1968.
11. See the analyses of agrarian revolt and banditry of R. Aya, *The Missed Revolution*, University of Amsterdam, Papers on European and Mediterranean Societies, 1975; H. Hess, *Mafia and Mafiosi*, Saxon House, 1973; and E. E. Malefakis, *Agrarian Reform and Peasant Revolution in Spain*, New Haven, Yale University Press, 1970.
12. On the inner cliques and clienteles of the PDC in post-war Italy see A. Zuckerman, *Political Clienteles in Power*, London and Beverly Hills, Sage, 1975. The description of the forces in the Spanish PD of the 1860s follows Díaz del Moral, *Historia*, chapter 2.
13. At least part of the variance and contradictory characterisations indicated above may be due to integral regional differentiation in patterns of stratification, as a detailed look at the research done in the area might reveal. For instance, a cursory view at regional variations might confirm that microsocial factors such as the results of an early attempt at agrarian reform or industrialisation are critical for subsequent processes of social transformation (e.g. cf. Galt's and Gilmore's research on Italy in this light. See Galt, 'Rethinking', and D. Gilmore, 'Patronage and Class Conflict in Southern Spain', *Man* (*N.S.*), **12**, 1977, pp. 446–58. See also D. Gil: ore, 'An-

thropology of the Mediterranean Area', *Annual Review of Anthropology*, **11**, 1982, pp. 175–205.

14. Díaz del Moral, *Historia*; Carr, *Spain*, chapter 1.

15. 'Amoral familism' is according to Edward C. Banfield the ethos that pervaded the behaviour of those Southern Italians he researched in the 1950s. Their behaviour followed the rule of maximising the material, short-term advantage of the nuclear family, while assuming all others will do likewise. See his *The Moral Basis of the Backward Society*, New York, Free Press, 1958, especially chapter 5. For some of the best research on the structural conditions of Mediterranean ideological constructs see Aya, *The Missed Revolution*; J. Schneider and P. Schneider, *Culture and Political Economy in Western Sicily*, New York, Academic Press, 1976; and S. Silverman's work, e.g. her 'The Italian Land Reform: Some Problems in the Development of a Cultural Tradition', *Anthropological Quarterly*, **44**, 1971, pp. 66–77.

16. D. Gilmore, 'Patronage and Class Conflict'.

17. H. Alavi, 'Peasant Classes and Primordial loyalties', *Journal of Peasant Studies*, **1**, 1973, pp. 23–65.

18. Silverman, 'The Italian Land Reform'.

19. A parallel line of inquiry might try to reduce the variety of forms of stratification to several structural arrangements (such as small and large land holding and lease of lands—including sharecropping—in addition to hired labour arrangements) and then attempt to relate political behaviour to class origins, probably along the path led by Juan Linz more than a decade ago. Still the contradictory traits with which this section started would still need to be explained in terms of the formation and 'reproduction' of such attitudes within the framework of those structural arrangements.

20. See Gilmore, 'Anthropology of the Mediterranean Area' and J. Boissevain, 'Toward a Social Anthropology of the Mediterranean', *Current Anthropology*, **20**, 1979, pp. 81–3.

21. Among descriptive analyses see, for example, J. Pitt-Rivers, *People of the Sierra*, New York, Criterion Books, 1954; and J. Boissevain, 'Poverty and Politics in a Sicilian Agrotown', *International Archives of Ethnography*, **50**, 1966, pp. 189–236.

22. The classification that follows has been adapted from L. Gallino, 'Italy', pp. 90–124 in S. Archer and S. Giner, (eds.), *Contemporary Europe: Class, Status, and Power*, London, Weidenfeld and Nicholson, 1980.

23. Description follows Hess, *Mafia*. For other works emphasising the minute social differentiation and hierarchisation of local social formations see F. M. Snowden, 'On the Social Origins of Agrarian Fascism in Italy', *Archives Européennes de Sociologie*, **13**, 1972, pp. 268–95; and Lison-Tolosona, *Belmonte de los Caballeros*, Oxford, Clarendon Press, 1966.

24. On the 'nominalist' and 'realist' approaches to social stratification see for instance J. Matras, *Social Inequality, Stratification, and Mobility*, Englewood Cliffs, Prentice Hall, chapters 5 to 7; D. Lockwood, 'Sources

of Variation in Working Class Images of Society', *Sociological Review*, **14**, 1966, pp. 249–67; and D. H. Wang, 'Social Inequality without Stratification', pp. 513–20 in C. S. Heller, *Structured Social Inequality*, New York, Macmillan, 1969. By adopting a nominalist perspective, the foregoing strata might be placed in the following classes: Upper class—*nobili*; upper middle class—*civili*, *professionisti* and *gabelotti*; lower middle class—*artigiani* and *massari*; upper lower class—*burgisi* and *mezzadri*; and lower lower class—*braccianti*, *caprai* and *pecoria*.

25. Hess, *Mafia*, p. 35.
26. See, for example, A. Blok, 'South Italian Agrotowns', *Comparative Studies in Society and History*, **11**, 1969, pp. 121–35. The historian Martin Clark has recently remarked in this connection that some of the Southern provinces have been and remained among the most urbanised in Italy. (See his *Modern Italy*).
27. The trend indicated here is not peculiar to Western Sicily. It was found also in Spain as shown in Pitt-Rivers' work, *The People of the Sierra*, although in the latter a greater congruence was found between residence patterns and behavioural styles.
28. See G. Lenski, *Power and Privilege*, MacGraw Hill, 1966.
29. Absenteeism of *latifondisti* controlling vast extensions of land and renting their estates to individuals who run them as if they were their own was a common phenomenon in Western Sicily from the nineteenth century onwards (Boissevain, 'Poverty', p. 206).
30. 'Contact with soil and animals is felt to be humiliating and unclean' (Hess, *Mafia*, p. 35).
31. 'Political careers were still founded on journalism, as in the days of Mussolini and Gramsci. Leading politicians, when asked to state their profession, proudly answered 'journalist'—in 1976 the Chamber of Deputies contained fifty-six 'journalists', including the Prime Minister, the secretary of the Communist Party, and the next President of the Republic' (Clark, *Modern Italy*, p. 367).
32. J. Pitt-Rivers, *The Fate of Schechem*, Cambridge University Press, 1977, chapter 2.
33. See J. Peristiany, *Honour and Shame: The Values of Mediterranean Society*, London, Weidenfeld and Nicholson, 1965; S. H. Brandes, *Metaphors of Masculinity*, Philadelphia, University of Pennsylvania Press, 1980; and Pitt-Rivers, *The Fate of Schechem*.
34. 'Physical violence is not thought to be a legitimate way to obtain one's ends, yet when his rights are infringed, a man is forced to stand up for himself under pain of appearing a coward' (Pitt-Rivers, *The Fate of Schechem*, p. 31).
35. For instance, 57 per cent of the general managers of Spanish ministries from 1938 to 1974 came from the so-called Grand Corps, which were in a sense a small group with routine contacts. Nevertheless, they still maintained clearly identified boundaries which led to identify powerholders as part of such categories as state attorneys, diplomats, fiscal inspectors, civil engineers, agricultural engineers, industrial engineers, naval engineers,

forestal engineers, military engineers, and so on (C. R. Alba, 'Spain after Franco'. Unpublished manuscript, 1979). This trait of narrow status segregation has been found not only among the upper strata but also among other sectors along the scale of stratification, as described above for Western Sicily.

36. See for instance V. Pérez Díaz, *Pueblos y clases sociales en el campo español*, Madrid, Siglo XXI, 1974; A. M. Calero, *Movimientos sociales en Andalucía (1820–1936)*, Madrid, Siglo XXI; C. Rossetti, 'The Ideology of Banditry', *Man (N.S.)*, **16**, 1981, pp. 158–60; J. M. Maravall, *El desarrollo económico y la clase obrera*, Barcelona, Ariel, 1970; and Aya, *The Missed Revolution*.

37. Attitudes of distrust towards others (such as assuming that people's nature is to take advantage of others), intensive envy, and moral justification of taking advantage of other's weaknesses have been typical of Mediterranean societies. (For Western Sicily see discussion in Schneider and Schneider, *Culture and Political Economy*.) That is, while people rely on neighbours' assistance and build reciprocity, at the same time, tensions and conflicts have emerged within the context of shared residence and adjacent fields. In consequence, secrecy concerning activities which are likely to give offense to others, and their avoidance, i.e., the minimisation of social encounters and creation of a category of people with whom one is not on talking terms, were used as strategies for reducing the likeness of conflict (E. Cohen, 'Who Stole the Rabbits: Crime, Dispute, and Social Control in an Italian Village', *Anthropological Quarterly*, **45**, 1972, pp. 1–14; and H. Pitkin, 'Mediterranean Europe', *Anthropological Quarterly*, **36**, 1963, pp. 120–9). Mechanisms like these, or, alternatively, ostentatious cordiality and hospitality, may be seen as indications of the wide extent of such intra-strata conflicts.

38. See S. N. Eisenstadt, 'The Structuring of Social Hierarchies in Comparative Perspective', in this book chapter 6.

39. The analytical approach to human civilisations developed by S. N. Eisenstadt allows to look at Europe from a global, comparative perspective. From such a perspective, the following cultural orientations stand out as typical of Europe: an emphasis on the autonomy of the cosmic, cultural and social orders; a high level of mutual relevance between them which was defined in terms of tension between the transcendental and mundane orders; the multiplicity and complexity of the ways of resolving this tension, either through 'this-worldly' (political and economic) or 'other-worldly' activities; a high level of activism and potential or actual commitment to broader groups and to the social and cosmic order; and the conception of a high degree of autonomous access of different groups and strata to these orders, to some degree countered by and in constant tension with, the strong emphasis on the mediation of such access by political actors and such institutions as the Church. (See e.g. S. N. Eisenstadt, 'Cultural Orientations and Centre-Periphery in Europe in a Comparative Perspective', in P. Torsvik, (ed.) *Mobilisation, Center-Periphery Structures and Nation-Building*, Bergen, University of Bergen Press.)

40. See Davis, *People of the Mediterranean*; and S. N. Eisenstadt and L.

Roniger, *Patrons, Clients and Friends. Interpersonal Relations and the Structure of Trust in Society*, pp. 50–81, Cambridge University Press, 1984.

41. On G. Foster's concept of the 'Image of Limited Good' as developed from his Mesoamerian fieldwork, see Foster, 'Peasant Society and the Image of Limited Good', *American Anthropologist*, **67**, 1965, pp. 293–315; idem, 'A Second Look at Limited Good', *Anthropological Quarterly*, **45**, 1972, pp. 57–64; and J. R. Gregory, 'Image of Limited Good or Expectation of Reciprocity?' *Current Anthropology*, **16**, 1975, pp. 73–92.

42. For bibliographical references on these see H. Driessen and D. Meertens, *A Selected Bibliography on Spanish Society*, University of Amsterdam Papers on European and Mediterranean Societies, 1976.

43. A usual Spanish pattern was to attempt to gain power and exclude opponents. When new elites replaced former incumbents to the political centre, they adopted exclusivist policies as the latter. When contesting elites could not or failed to take over power, often they opted to emigrate, expecting to return only to accede to central positions. In Italy, such tendencies were typical only of the period that preceded Italian unification and during the Fascist period.

8 The American system of stratification: some notes towards understanding its symbolic and institutional concomitants

Adam Seligman

The study of stratification in America: the current state of analysis

The United States, as has often been noted, is unique among Western industrialised societies in the openness of its class structure, its relatively high degree of inter-strata mobility (both real and perceived) and the lack of any clearly definable symbolism or ideology of class membership and 'affective' class commitments among different status incumbents.[1] These unique characteristics of the American stratification system have furthermore, since Sombart's early work been linked to American 'exceptionalism' and the failure of socialism to emerge as a strong political movement.[2]

Indeed the close connection between the unique determinants of the American system of stratification and the broader characteristics of the American political order was a phenomena noted by none other than Alexis de Tocqueville in the early nineteenth century. For De Tocqueville democracy itself was less a political regime and more a social condition of equality. In his *Democracy in America* he speaks of democracy as a condition of class, or rather classlessness—intimating that the assumption of power on the part of this class rests on the infusion of democratic 'moeurs' and laws within the body politic.[3]

De Tocqueville's thought moved in a direction which would provide the focus for social research a century and a half after his death. For a while originally equating 'la democratie' with 'le peuple' (the latter being all classes of citizens) De Tocqueville moved to the notion of a correspondence between democracy and 'le mouvement'.[4] The notion of democracy as movement, as a mechanism, essentially of mobility is brought out clearly in his working drafts for the 1835 text of Democracy in America where he states:

That constantly renewed agitation introduced by democratic government into political life passes, then into civil society ... Democracy ... spreads throughout the body social a restless activity, superabundant force, and energy never found elsewhere, which however little favoured by circumstances can do wonders.[5]

While in later writing he would free his concept of democracy from the New World context, the intimate connection between the social state of democracy and of an equality of social condition where all have equal life chances and there exists no effective class divisions has remained a hallmark in the study of American society.

The sociological analysis of stratification in the United States has been an ongoing enterprise for many decades and the body of literature devoted to its many facets is immense.[6] As a detailed review of this corpus is not our intention we will make do with an analytic review of a number of representative examples. In noting the work of some of the major contributors to the field we will *inter alia* concentrate on some of the major analytic *loci* of its research—its perspectives and problems.

The major characteristics of this research have been a pervasive stress on mobility, on a broad based middle-class and the lack of any cognitive or affective class consciousness among status incumbents. Most studies have stressed the elements of status continuum, that is the gradual, 'natural' transitions from strata to strata rather than the existence of structured hierarchies within the social system. Classical studies such as those by G. Lenski, O. Cox, J. Cuber and W. Kennedy, A. Kornhauser have all abjured the notion of class structure in favour of more multidimensional concepts of status and labile notions of the structural characteristics of class and strata.[7] These studies have been followed by those such as of Blau and Duncan which reject discrete classes in favour of indexes on a continuum of education, occupation and prestige.[8]

This mode of analysis achieved its most salient expression in the work of Warner and Lunt who made the perception of status (i.e. the perception of the basis of inequality) the dominant mode of social research in lieu of a more class orientated analysis (stressing the structural characteristics of strata differentiation).[9] Not surprisingly, studies such as these have stressed the subjective component of the perception of individual strata differences, a conception well illustrated in the work of Nelson and Laswell who claim:

Each individual may have a variety of social classes attributed to him, dependent on the attributor and the situation as defined by the attributor; there is no rigid framework which can be laid over society by which to draw on absolute social class hierarchy; that is no single absolute or real class construct that social class is dependent not on a series of variables advanced by a researcher and rightly or wrongly manipulated by him, but rather on three crucial turning points; time, space and perception. In effect individuals may have different social classes similar to their different social roles and the class to which they will be assigned is a function of this situation, the time and the perception not on an absolute set of pre-ordained variables.[10]

The growth of research oriented towards mapping out subjective attitudes towards class in the United States involved *inter alia* a plethora of empirical studies on the existence or lack of an explicit class consciousness among status incumbents. Among those who carried out some of the most fruitful research in this field was Werner Landecker who published in the sixties a number of empirical studies on the perception of class boundaries and on the different modes of class consciousness. His findings are relevant to our own analysis as they present interesting insights on both the perception of status incumbency and on the objective referents of such perception. Thus for instance in his study on class boundaries he found that while class boundaries did exist in the United States the social structure as a whole was not characterised by any clearly definable structural divisions. In so far as he pointed to the existence of a division between a social elite and the mass of the populace he effectively negated those theorists of a 'radical continuum' (who claimed the existence of no structural breaks). On the other hand, his findings on the high degree of social coherence, covering a wide range of strata and sub-strata point to the inability to characterise America in 'straight' class–structural terms taken from other social contexts.

Similarly his substantive research on class crystallisation and class consciousness has pointed to the inadvisability of conflating cognitive and affective modes of class consciousness. That is to say that self-placement in a class is not always synonymous with class solidarity, that a discernment of class differences does not necessarily imply the assertion of class boundaries and that an identification of personal with class interests does not of itself lead to hostility towards other classes.[11]

It is however precisely in the attempt to explain the complex patterning of subjective attitudes towards status placement that research into the American stratification system has run into a number of not inconsequential problems. Indeed over the trajectory of research into the American stratification system, analysts have met with increasing difficulties in breaking down the stratification system to its different components. Such difficulty was already envinced in L. Warner's six fold division of upper-upper, lower-upper, upper-middle, lower-middle, upper-lower, lower-lower 'classes' and the inherent problem of relating membership in any one category to the ubiquitous 'common man'.[12] The complexity (and ultimate limitations) of such an approach is felt in statements such as the following:

> If it is discovered that a person belongs to the Country Club in Jonesville, the chances seem favorable for placement somewhere above Common Man, since over half of the known membership is above the level. But when we learn this person is a member of the Western Star, where almost all the known membership is lower-middle, and we later find out that he is a Royal Kinsman, the chances are overwhelming that his real placement will be lower-middle—lower-middle because the previously established lower limit of the Country Club is lower-middle and the upper limits of the Royal Kinsman are lower-middle, while Western Star is entirely lower-middle and has no membership below that class.[13]

Such classification is further complicated by the fact that the coordinates of this system were attained by a multivariable analysis of occupation, income source, house type, dwelling area, education and amount of income—each category given to a seven fold differentiation. The complexity of this system of classification is if anything only heightened in Coleman and Rainwater's albeit penetrating study of perceptions of social stratification, published a generation later.[14] Here a six or seven fold categorisation gives way to a thirteen fold one, where upper-class Americans are subdivided into upper and lower upper, upper-middle upper Americans into upper middle elite, upper middle core and upper middle marginal and so on through middle-class middle, working-class middle and lower-class Americans (and this before the emergence of the 'Yuppy'). Indeed Coleman and Rainwater's study stresses precisely the multi-level hierarchies within the American system of social stratification. They (and others) however do so in such a way that leads us back to Nelson and Laswell's major point: Do these multiplex divisions reflect the real perception of status incongruities or the needs of social researchers to order what are in essence highly amorphous, labile and individual perceptions of class in America? For what is overwhelmingly clear from the above is that as opposed to Europe, America is characterised by a lack of any perception of class *per se* as opposed to more group based orientations and attitudes.

One of the important characteristics of all the above noted studies has of course been their failure (following in the tradition of the Warner school) to employ economic and political bases for class membership. This lacuane has been noted by Former and Putman, who moreover attempt in their recent article a tentative beginning at an objective analysis of American working class positioning.[15] Using the conception of a segmented labour market, presenting unequal structural conditions in different employment sectors they too attempt to deal with the lack of a class solidarity among blue-collar American workers. Dividing workers first into self-employed, skilled and semi-skilled and then over core and peripheral industries, their study brings to light the discrepancy between given economic/structural condtions (which in the case of skilled workers and the non-skilled in core industries are similar) and the perception of social needs and status placement. Thus while stressing the given conditions of structural inequality their study lends added weight to the mass of existing evidence on the lack of effective commitments, modes of solidarity or of an active class consciousness (in 'Lukacsian' terms of a 'class for itself') among American working class status incumbents.

Concomitant with the growth and sophistication of empirical studies on both the perception of class in the United States and its structural characteristics has been the reappraisal of the earlier 'opportunity' theorists of the American social system. In this general reappraisal of notions of an all pervasive 'openness' of the American social system Lipset and Bendix's famous study of *Social Mobility in Industrial Societies* has played a major role.[16] The two major analytic *loci* of their work were: (a) that substantial difference in patterns of mobility between America and other industrial societies do not in fact exist; and (b) that it is impossible to isolate either specific patterns of mobility or the perception thereof in the United States from society's central values of equality and individualism.

Following on these insights, researchers have gone on to question many of the long held beliefs about social mobility in the United States. Thus studies such as Karabel's have pointed to the discrepancy between high wage levels, relative to Europe and the rate of increase in real terms—which may in fact not have been higher than in Europe.[17] Similarly it has been noted that inequality both within the wage-earning class and between it and the employer class may have been higher in the United States than in Europe.[18] Even that paradigm of mobility theory, the 'frontier thesis', as used by Sombart has come under attack.[19] Finally, studies by Therstrom, Miller and Erikson have all led to the realisation that mobility rates in all industrialised countries are similar with no marked difference in the United States.[20]

Summing up the different research perspectives noted above a seemingly paradoxical situation emerges of the existence of deep rooted inequalities in a social system which is nevertheless perceived in terms of class openness, opportunity, mobility and the lack of rigidly defined, immutable social hierarchies.

In many ways this fact leads us back to De Tocqueville and his assessment of the intimate relation between the American social and political systems. For the perception of the social system was then and is today inherently of a political nature. Yet the former has changed radically in the 150 years since the publication of *Democracy in America*. The agricultural society he surveyed and upon which he based his analysis of American mobility and structural openness has given way to an industrial one, the broad base of small freeholders has given way to an industrial working class. Yet the political system has remained intact and the identity between democracy as a social mechanism (albeit of increasingly undefined nature in light of recent studies) and democracy as a political concept have been maintained. One of the most salient derivatives of this identity has been felt in the lack of strong class based political movements or parties in the United States. The early granting of universal male suffrage (predating the emegence of a large-scale proletariat) precluded not only a working class politics, but the need for middle-class revolutions and a class consciousness as well. As a result not only did the working class fail to develop broadbased and effective political organisations but such organisations and a concomitant sense of class identity and politics were superfluous for the middle classes as well. This lack of political consciousness of class (in any of its dimensions) and its concomitant models of mobilisation and organisation of class based action has provided a subject of much analysis and research. In the main however, these have concentrated less on the lack of class based political action among middle class groups and more on the failure of the American working classes to pursue their interests along class lines. The main parameters of this debate have therefore been on the failure of socialism in the United States—the case of American 'exceptionalism'.

In the vast amount of material published on the subject of 'American exceptionalism' a number of analytic points have come over the years to gain greater and greater weight. Thus, beyond the specific analysis of the American stratification system, political factors, the debates around the cooptation of the socialist leadership or of the frontier as a safety valve; an appreciation of the unique constellation of value orientations or ideology and a specific set of institutional features has emerged as providing a crucial perspective on the American phenomenon. One of the most important works in this genre is S. M. Lipset's paper on the 'Sources of Working Class Politics', which synthetically integrates different elements of analysis—hierarchic status relations, feudal remnants and political rights with class-based ideologies, working class organisation and legitimacy to explain the different trajectories of working class politics in different societies.[21] In his work Lipset clarifies the role of different value orientations in society and their effect on the structuring of socialist impingement and of society's response. In the case of America this perspective leads to a re-evaluation of such factors as: the lack of a feudal heritage, the early achievement of political equality, the specific patterns of status orientations, the relations between socialist elites and organised labour and the unique nature of the American ideological system—as prime components in any explanation of the particular form of class action taken in the United States.

Indeed continued work on the nature of working class mobilisation in the United States has repeatedly shown the link between the lack of a socialist electorate and a very particular patterning of structural and orientational factors. A dynamic further exemplified by the fact that along with the failure of socialism, the United States has been characterised by a relatively low percentage of unionisation (less than one quarter of the industrialised labour force after World War I), that is by what has been the traditional mode for the realisation of collective demands by the wage earning class.[22] As with American exceptionalism in the case of socialism, this fact too has been related to such factors as class-composition of the working class, the power of the employer class and most centrally the mobility of the stratification system. However, and most importantly research has continually pointed here as well to the specific characteristics of American historical development such as: 'the inter-class character of the American revolution, the radical anti-monopoly critique of the capitalism and the nationalist impact of the Civil War', as factors explaining the low level of unionisation in the United States of America.[23] Moreover certain researchers, notably Shalev and Korpi have suggested that both factors of the failure of socialism and of unionisation are inexorably linked, with the latter playing a possibly causal role in the former.[24] These authors further stress the inability of reducing patterns of class action in general and among the American working class in particular to structural factors (class composition, employer power) alone.

Concurring in this judgement we would stress even further the need for isolating the precise role different value orientations and ideological constructs played in shaping the particular patterning of structural factors. Thus for example the case made to explain the failure of socialism and unionisation revolves, in part, around the analysis of the power of the employer class and their tactics of both repression and cooptation of socialist and union leadership. Such a perspective would gain in cogency were it related to an analysis of the specific models of elite formation in the United States and the nature of their analytic characteristics. These moreover, were themselves linked to the basic symbolic and structural framework of the American social centre and the particular nature of its crystallisation. Both facts, it should be noted are coming more and more into the awareness of social scientists dealing with the different problems and perspectives attendant on the study of stratification in the United States. Thus Shalev and Korpi themselves note that the 'limits of structural explanation are indicated when we consider the extent to which the outcomes of past religious and nation building conflicts have continued to colour the organisation of the industrial working class.'[25] Their own insights, which implicitly recognise the importance of such factors as political participation, the structuring of collective boundaries (and 'the particular visions of society' which inform such structuring) as well as competing class allegiances serve yet again to heighten awareness of how the unique configuration of social structuration together with a particular value system (containing unique definitions of membership and citizenship) is central to understanding the failure of working class Americans to develop affective class-based identities and commitment, and to articulate them politically.

The present context of analysis

We maintain that just as the afore-mentioned insights have proved valuable in explaining the phenomenon of American exceptionalism they also provide valuable guide-posts towards a renewed and somewhat revised study of the unique characteristics of the American system of social stratification. In the following we will attempt to locate a number of additional variables which influenced the particular structuring of the American stratification system. Taking as our starting point the low level of class identification and of explicitly articulated class based protest or class symbolism in protest we will attempt to widen existing perspectives on the absence of a 'class consciousness' or identification in the United States. This, through a study of the major symbolic and institutional characteristics which influenced the structuring of the perception, articulation and organisation of class interests. In slightly different terms, through a study of how a particular patterning of ideas on the nature of the social order channelled and continues to channel interest motivated action.

Our undertaking of such a mode of inquiry into the determinants of class formation in the United States is, it should be noted, explicitly informed by Weber's famous dictum: 'that interests (material and ideal), not ideas, directly govern man's conduct. Yet very frequently the 'world images' that have been created by 'ideas' have, like switchmen, determined the tracks along which action has been pushed by the dynamic of interests.'[26] Indeed the following is a preliminary and tentative attempt to indicate the general lines along which a concrete analysis based on the above premise may be conducted.

As such we will primarily be concerned with a critical evaluation of how a number of ideas, or more specifically, basic assumptions on different aspects of the social order tended to influence the definition and perception of the social structure in general and the pursuit of class interests within it in particular.

Of particular relevance in this context was the existence within the collective of a number of dominant assumptions on the nature of collective solidarity, the terms of national identity, the broader purpose of collective goals and the modes of political legitimation. Here a number of features emerge as unique to the American socio-political order. These were: its particular conceptions of individualism as opposed to collectivism and the anti-statist orientations which evolved in American society, as well as the particular structures of American nationalism, neither primordial nor rooted in an organic historical development, with its own unique ideological crystallisation and the strong future orientation of American values and beliefs.

The above orientations and the nature of their constellation in early American society was reflected in the characteristics of the American social centre and of its elite groups; both of which played a major role in structuring the fundamental terms of class consciousness and social action in society.

Characteristics of the American centre

The American centre manifested a number of unique characteristics, both symbolic and structural in nature, which together tended to define its uniqueness from other centres and which contributed to the course taken by the structuring of social hierarchies therein. Its principle defining traits were its openness; its lack of distinction from the periphery; an early separation of powers between Church and State and the development following the Revolution of a legal-rational system of legitimation endowed with a degree of charisma. With the above, orientations to achievement and equality stood at the centre of the American socio-political consensus.

Following on the symbolic attributes of the centre are a number of structural characteristics which, while serving to define the set of centre–periphery relations had as well a crucial impact on the development of class formation in the United States. Among these was the particular structure of direct and unmediated access to centre orders by all members of the collective. Moreover, in America the issues of legitimation of political power and the crystallisation of collective identity, were resolved before the crystallisation of the political centre. As a result, the problems faced by the centre were in the main organisational and regulatory in nature.

Concomitant with the importance of centre structures on the development of class formation in the United States was, as mentioned above, the particular structure and characteristics of the major elite groups. These shared certain symbolic assumptions and organisational characteristics which proved of great importance in the development of social hierarchies and the pursuit of class interests.

Characteristics of elites

Among the major symbolic characteristics of American elite groups the most important were:

— The open potentiality of all social actors to become elites and of different groups of elites to articulate orientations in all spheres of social life;
— The interweaving of orientations among and between different elite groups. Unlike Europe, there existed no separation or segregation of orientations among different sets of elites;
— Different groups of elites were accepted as legitimate articulators of social models and desiderata in the various spheres of social life (legal, economic, social and religious).

The symbolic definitions of legitimate spheres of activity by American elites was itself tied to their organisational and structural characteristics. Namely, their autonomous nature, relatively free of rigid social structures and frameworks—a characteristic of religious, intellectual, entrepreneurial and political elites.

Related to both the interweaving of orientation and symbolic non-differentiation between elites, was the relative weakness of elite specialisation. Although there was some degree of specialisation among entrepreneurial elites, this was not matched by a similar tendency in the political realm. This was combined with a high degree of structural weakness and lack of organisational strength among elites, especially political ones. Comparison with Europe, where political elites tended to extent their influence over broad realms of social life, elucidates the importance of this characteristic in structuring of American political elites.

Finally, there existed no strict distinction between centre and periphery elites, a feature concomitant with the inter-penetration of both and their relative lack of distinction.

Value orientations, class formation and the perception of social hierarchies

The importance of the above noted symbolic assumptions, and structural characteristics of the American centre and of its elites in influencing the modes of perception and articulation of class identity and interests is to be found in a number of overlapping if analytically distinct realms.

Value orientations

Its influence was felt foremost in structuring the major reference orientations of collectivity members towards the basic terms of solidarity and membership. For just as a certain moral element was a constitutive factor in American politics, so were political factors a central focus for national identity. As an immigrant society, of diverse religious faiths and with divergent cultural backgrounds the American conception of membership and collective identity became based on its political ideals as opposed to more primordial criteria. The result of this has been that 'Americanism is to the American not a tradition, or a territory, not what France is to a Frenchman or England to an Englishman, but a doctrine—what socialism is to a socialist'.[27] It is adherence to this doctrine, to the codes of civil religion and to the political ideals articulated and instituted with the republic, that defines the parameters of American collective identity. Thus throughout history, becoming an American has meant becoming a believer in this civil religion.

Moreover and intimately embedded in this civil religion were the different values of equality and achievement. Rooted in the English radical tradition of common law and natural rights on the one hand and the religious heritage of dissenting Puritanism on the other, and as expressed in both the Declaration of Independence and the Constitution—the symbolic and institutional *loci* of the American system —these became constant referents of American national ideology and identity. Thus the early linkage of individual salvation with the accomplishments of the collective as a whole (which characterised the Puritan 'Errand Into the Wilderness') became articulated over time as the interweaving of individual fullfilment with broader social goals. Indeed and as pointed out by S. M. Lipset, the very legitimacy of the early republic, and hence of the use of power, rested on this very particular interpretation of individual fullfilment.[28]

Class formation

The structuring of class identity and membership during the process of industrialisation was affected by the above orientations, a dynamic whose unique features can best be seen in the case of the working class. For the particular form of working class integration into national life saw their acceptance of (and by) the pervading terms of national identity and collective membership with the resulting failure of the American working class to develop a specific sense of 'class consciousness', belonging or commitment.

Lacking either primordial orientations or roots in feudal *Standen* there was in the United States never a problem of integration of the working class into national life. Working class integration both *de jure* and *de facto* into collective life was never an issue of intense conflict, as opposed to the often violent confrontations engendered by demands of the working class for broadening the system of distributive justice and opening greater venues of access to major markets and resources.[29] As a result there never developed that type of class-consciousness, crosscutting national/territorial identity—a characteristic of class crystallisation in Europe—which played a salient role in structuring the perception of social hierarchies there as well as the politics of the pursuit of class interest. In so doing, it played a major role in both the growth of socialism as well as the development of a high rate of unionisation in these countries.

On a more structural level this dynamic was a derivative of the relative openness of the American social system, not simply, in terms of the different modes of generational, geographic and status mobility, but in terms of access to major markets and resources (as well as in terms of resource convertibility).

On a political level the low level of class consciousness in the United States (not only of the working class, but of all status groups, except for certain groups within the upper class) was a direct result of this openness. Whereas the monopolisation of access to major social centres and markets led in the European context to struggles of emerging social classes to gain access and control of the centre, in the United States by contrast, both the failure of such monopolisation to occur together with the lack of any significant symbolic of institutional differentiation between centre and periphery led to a consequent de-emphasis on a class or strata directed definition of social identities.

The perception of social hierarchies

A further and important corolary of the above was felt in the perception of social hierarchies and status differentiation. Interesting in this context and beyond the importance of both the facts and 'myth' of social mobility as an expression of the lack of any rigidly defined hierarchic or ascriptive status notions within the collective is what Lee Rainwater has termed 'validating' activities.[30] That is, 'activities that confirm a person's sense of himself as a full and reconsised member of his society, resonating with his sense of inner needs'; activities which 'achieve a sense of concordance between social placement and personal identity'. In fact, sociological studies such as those of Baltzell on the historical development of entrepreneurial elites in Boston and Philadelphia or of Rainwater, emphasise the continual influence of the above orientations, which act as basic social and symbolic premises through which people define both their individual and collective existence.[31]

What has been termed the myth of social mobility is, as these studies have shown, in essence an expression of the perceived lack of ascriptive status attributes and of the basic 'openness' of the social system.

Continued evidence of this very particularly American mode of perceiving social hierarchies is evinced in yet another major arena—that of race relations, where ascriptive criteria for membership did play an important role. In a recent and indepth study of the Boston bussing/school integration crisis A. Lukas has made more than evident how the issue of class was a hidden feature in the struggle between black and white communities in Boston's inner city.[32] This feature of racial conflict, hiding conflict between different status groups was already hinted at by Lipset and Bendix in the sixties and is congruent with the overriding notions of membership and collective identity in America as presented above. For a while ascriptive criteria did block paths to mobility as well as participation and acceptance in the centre in the case of blacks, what is important to note is that in so doing it tended continually to obscure class conflicts rooted in differential and hierarchical patterning among status groups.

Elites and the organisation of protest

Of course the entrenchment of the above orientations and perceptions within the collective did not preclude the articulation and organisation of periphery protest against deep-seated inequalities within the socioeconomic structure. However, here too the organisation of class interest was well as the dynamics of centre–periphery interaction were structured by many characteristics of the centre and especially of the elites active in society. In the development of different types of protest to widen avenues of access to the centres of resource or prestige, or to re-evaluate the system of distributive justice the analytic characteristics of the different elite groups played a significant role. Thus the potentiality of all individuals to become political elites, the open access to centre orders and the almost non-existent differentiation between the centre and the periphery militated against the development of alternate political structures, *loci* of power, of mobilisation or of identity. One of the additional reasons for this particular dynamic was the singular propensity of different elites (entrepreneurial, intellectual or religious) at one time or another, to become political elites, concentrate on a specific issue or cause and then revert back to their earlier social role. This led to the great degree of organisational diversity and weakness among protest movements, and their consequent failure to articulate a politics of class interest in opposition to existing social cultural and political models. Indeed the example *par excellence* of this phenomena was the American socialist movement which never moved beyond the basic assumptions of the given social order (in either its symbolic premises or concrete demands).

On a more concrete level this was felt in both the incorporation of socialist elites into the existing political frameworks as well as in the unique nature of labour–management relations in the United States. For what has often been termed the cooptation of union leadership was in essence, as shown by studies such as Laslett's, an integration of union elites into the decision making process and into participation in the constructing of some of the major realms of social existence.[33]

Yet another arena shaped by the characteristics of elite groups was the realm of party organisation. For as has been recognised since the time of De Tocqueville, parties in the United States were always formed with relative ease and with high rates of mass participation.

They were moreover, throughout most of the nineteenth century, less like large bureaucratic structures and more akin to social movements, tending to define themselves and be defined as carriers of social progress.

This fact has been seen as important by some researchers, notably David Kamens who claims that the historical characteristics of American political parties was a crucial element in the failure of socialism there.[34] American parties, developing before the institutionalisation of a strong central state apparatus, were thus able to claim legitimacy as representatives of the whole nation. (A representation monopolised by the state in those collectivities where the historical sequencing saw the development of parties after the crystallisation of a strong centralised state, as in Europe). This particular claim to legitimacy together with the dominant orientation of American parties to 'patronage' as opposed to 'policy' resulted in a political rhetoric which avoided appealing to class symbols and interests and stressed in their stead the representation of broad interests and social groups within a populistic ethic.[35] While for Kammens the crucial variable in this development is that of the historical timing of party development, it is important to note that the above dynamic rested as well on the open nature of elite organisation. The ease with which, in David Kamen's terms, 'outsiders became insiders' was itself predicated on the open characteristic of elite groups in society as well as the symbolic and structural openness of the centre.

Of final and important note is the intimate linkage of the above to one of the major value referents of American society. For what can be seen from the above is not only the difficulty of pursuing specific interests in terms of class symbols within the context of American politics but something of perhaps greater import. For the popular and populistic rhetoric of American political parties, claiming to represent the interests of the whole of society constituted in essence a legitimation of the social order in universalistic terms (given the particular, open, non-ascriptive nature of membership, solidarity and citizenship in the United States)[36], rooted in the same revolutionary *Erlebnis* of socialism itself. Thus the lack of a feudal heritage (with its inherent symbolic and structural limitations on membership in the collectivity), the early timing of mass enfranchisment together with the singular lack of distinction between the social centre and the periphery resulted in the essential 'irrelevancy' of socialist legitimation and indeed, of any class based party structure or ideology. As a result the major characteristics of the socialist movement (a strong future orientation, messianism, this-worldliness and emphasis on active participation and commitment to the social order—which were also its legitimising framework) were in the case of the United States characteristic of most political parties which in essence 'pre-empted' socialist claims to legitimation in universalistic terms.

The pursuit of class interests in socialist terms was therefore 'stymied' in the United States in two of its most important 'moments', either as pursuit of the specific interests of the working class, which was a decidedly uncongenial mode of political practice given the dominant models of political discourse; or as a universalistic/utopian vision, which was also precluded by the early 'appropriation' of this vision by existing social groups and political parties.

The pursuit of class interest as well as its very perception rested in the United States on both the symbolic premises and structural characteristics of the centre as well as on the nature of the major social elites and especially the political ones. This insight should provide however no more than a starting point for more detailed and comparative work into the role of some of the variables mentioned above in the structuring of social hierarchies in both America and other social formations.

Concluding remarks and research perspectives

Summing up the above, we would argue that the study of the perception of social hierarchies and of class formation, and the pursuit of class interests in the United States, as in any other collectivity, must take account of the dominant cultural orientations articulated in society and of their institutional embodiments. For the particular patterning of major cultural orientations, the characteristics of elite groups who carried them and the modes of their institutionalisation in society tended to define different aspects of social identity and of social action.

More concretely, we have sought to relate one of the most salient features of the American stratification system, namely its lack of any rigid status demarcation lines, with the basic patterning of cultural orientations, symbolic and institutional orders of the centre and the structuring of the major elite groups in society. For it was to a major extent the unique constellation of these factors which had an important influence on the structuring of status hierarchies. Of no less importance was their effect on the manner of the representation and articulation of status differentiation among status incumbants as expressed in the terms of collective membership, commitment to the basic orders of the centre and of the access granted social groups to major institutional markets and resources.

Among the major cultural orientations which influenced the concrete dynamics of collectivity structuring were the major assumptions on trust, the regulation of power, the legitimation of social hierarchies and of major institutional realms, as well as those on the broader purpose and meaning of collective goals.[37] These are moreover rooted, as in other societies, in a set of assumptions on the nature of the cosmic and social order and of their inter-relation. Although the framework of the present study precludes a detailed analysis of the latter, three major orientations can be seen as characterising the overarching set of symbolic premises incorporated in the structures and institutions of the American centre. These were an emphasis on an interweaving of this-wordly and other-worldly modes of salvation, with a marked emphasis on this worldly activities. This resulted in soteriological meaning attributed to economic activity, an idealisation of the political sphere and an extensive collective participation and responsibility to the political and cultural orders. There was as well a great deal of individual commitment to the centre. Enshrined in the early covenants of Puritan communities and related to the strong messianic perception of the colonial endeavour, this committment continued to characterise different stages of American nation-formation. Finally through the process of mutual impingement of conflicting religious elites, the early Puritan stress on the direct, autonomous and unmediated nature of access of the individual to the transcendental centre, was given a political articulation in the form of direct access to the socio-political centre.[38]

The present study has stressed one aspect of the way these orientations played a role in the structuring of social action and institution in the United States—in the main through the activities of different groups of social elites who articulated them. By bringing these perspectives of symbolic orientations and elite interaction together with an analysis of the specificity of the American centre and its relation with the periphery (of impingement and response, penetration and protest) a new direction is opened for the further study of stratification in the United States and other societies.

In the above, our focus has been on only a few of the major principles of strata formation, namely, the criteria effecting perceptions of class interests and class configurations. We have shown that these were informed by the symbolic orientations and the patterns of interaction followed by elites in the United States. A major task for future research along these perspectives would be to address other major principles of strata formation. Thus, for example, it would be important to show how the concrete models of class formation which developed in the nineteenth century were affected by the particular pattern of social mobility in America; or, alternatively, how the criteria for differential evaluation of status positions was structured by the fundamental assumptions on the nature of equality there. These are perspectives which we hope to have opened here and which would be enriched by informing further research with an appreciation of those symbolic and institutional factors presented above.

Notes

1. See S. M. Lipset and R. Bendix, *Social Mobility in Industrial Societies*, Berkeley, University of California Press, 1960; and S. M. Lipset, *The First New Nation: The U.S. In Historical and Comparative Perspective*, London, Heinemann, 1964.
2. W. Sombart, *Why is there no socialism in the United States*, New York, M. B. Sharpe Inc., 1976; S. M. Lipset, 'Why No Socialism in the United States', in S. Bialer and S. Sluzman, (eds.), *Sources of Contemporary Radicalism*, New York, Columbia University Press, 1977; S. M. Lipset, 'American "Exceptionalism" in North American Perspective: Why the U.S. has withstood the worldwide socialist movement', in F. M. Adams, (ed.), *The Idea of America*, Cambridge, Harvard University Press, 1977.
3. A. De Tocqueville, *Democracy in America*, New York, Vintage Press, 1966.
4. S. Schleifer, *The Making of Tocqueville's Democracy in America*, Chapel Hill, University of North Carolina Press, 1980.
5. *Ibid.*, p. 260.
6. H. Pfautz, 'The Current Literature on Social Stratification: Critique and Bibliography', *American Journal of Sociology*, **58** 1953, pp. 391–418.
7. G. E. Lenski, 'American Social Classes: Statistical Strata or Social Groups', *American Journal of Sociology*, **50**, 1952, pp. 139–44; idem, 'Status Crystallization: A Nonvertical Dimension of Social Status', *American Sociological Review*, **19**, 1954, pp. 405–13; O. Cox, *Caste, Class, Race*, New York, Monthly Review Press, 1948; J. Cuber and W. Kennedy, *Social Stratification in the U.S.A.*, New York, Appelton Century-Crofts, 1954; A. Kornhauser, 'Analysis of Class Structure of Contemporary American Society. Psychological Bases of Class Division', chapter 2, in G. W. Hartman and T. Newcomb, (eds.), *Industrial Conflict*, New York, Cordon, 1939.
8. P. Blau, and O. D. Duncan, *The American Occupational Structure*, New York, John Wiley, 1967.
9. L. Warner and P. Lunt, *The Status System of a Modern Community*, New Haven, Yale University Press, 1942; L. Warner, *Social Class in America The Evaluation of Status*, New York, Harper and Row, 1960.
10. H. H. Nelson and T. E. Laswell. 'Status Indices, Social Stratification and Social Class', *Society and Social Research*, **44**, 1960, pp. 412–13. See also E. E. Nelson, 'Status Inconsistency: Its Objective and Subjective Components', *The Sociological Quarterly*, **14**, 1973, pp. 2–18.
11. W. Landecker, 'Class Boundaries', *American Sociological Review*, **25**, 1960,

pp. 868–77; W. Landecker, 'Class Crystallization and Class Consciousness', *American Review*, 28, 1963, pp. 219–29.

12. Warner, *Social Class*.

13. *Ibid.*, p. 94.

14. R. Coleman and L. Rainwater, *Social Standing in America New Dimensions of Class*, New York, Basic Books, 1978.

15. W. Former, B. Putman, 'Economic Cleavages in the American Working Class', *British Journal of Sociology*, Vol. 36(1).

16. Lipset and Bendix, *Social Mobility*.

17. J. Karabel, 'The Reasons Why', *New York Review of Books*, 25, 1979, pp. 26–7.

18. C. T. Husbands, 'Editor's Introductory Essay', in W. Sombart, *Why is there No Socialism in the U.S.A.*, New York, M. G. Sharpe, 1976.

19. R. Hofstadter and S. Lipset, (eds.), *Turner and Sociology of the Frontier*, New York, Basic Books, 1968.

20. S. Thernstrom, 'Socialism and Social Mobility', pp. 509–27 in J. Laslett and S. Lipset, *Failure of a Dream? Essays in the History of American Socialism*, New York, Anchor Books, 1974; S. M. Miller, 'Comparative Social Mobility', *Current Sociology*, 9, 1960, pp. 1–89; and R. Erikson, 'Patterns of Social Mobility', pp. 171–204 in R. Scase, (ed.), *Readings in the Swedish Class Structure*, Oxford, Pergamon Press, 1976.

21. S. M. Lipset, 'Radicalism or Reformism: The Sources of Working-Class Politics', Presidential Address presented at 1982 American Political Science Association Annual Meeting.

22. M. Shalev and W. Korpi, 'Working Class Mobilization and American Exceptionalism', *Economic and Industrial Democracy*, 1, 1980, pp. 31–61, esp. p. 32.

23. A. Dawley, *Class and Community: The Industrial Revolution in Lynn*, Cambridge, Harvard University Press, 1976, p. 239.

24. Shalev and Korpi, 'Working Class', pp. 52–5.

25. *Ibid.*, p. 53.

26. M. Weber, 'The Social Psychology of World Religions', p. 280, in H. H. Gerth and P. W. Mills, (eds.), *From Max Weber. Essays in Sociology*, New York, Oxford University Press, 1946.

27. L. Sampson, 'American As Surrogate Socialism', p. 426, in J. Laslett and S. M. Lipset, (eds.), *Failure of a Dream*, New York, Doubleday, 1974.

28. Lipset, *The First New Nation*.

29. Lipset, 'Radicalism or Reformism'.

30. L. Rainwater, *What Money Buys: Inequality and the Social Meaning of Income*, New York, Basic Books, 1974.

31. E. O. Baltzell, *Puritan Boston and Quaker Philadelphia*, New York, Free Press, 1979.

32. J. A. Lukas, *Common Ground: A Turbulent Decade in the Lives of Three American Families*, New York, Knopf, 1985.

33. This point is made clear in the development of collective bargaining and the importance of contractual agreement in American labour-management

relations. J. Laslett, *Labor and the Left. A Study of Socialist and Radical Influences in the American Labor Movements, 1881—1924*, New York, Basic Books, 1970.

34. D. Kamens, 'The Importance of Historical Sequencing: Party Legitimacy in the U.S. and Europe'. Paper presented at the American Sociological Association, 1985 Meetings.

35. M. Schefter, 'Party and Patronage: Germany, England and Italy', *Politics and Society*, 7, 1977, pp. 403–51.

36. S. N. Eisenstadt, *Revolutions and the Transformation of Societies*, New York, Free Press, 1978.

37. S. N. Eisenstadt, 'The Structuring of Social Hierarchies in Comparative Perspective', in this book, chapter 6.

38. For a more detailed discussion and elaboration of these themes see S. N. Eisenstadt, 'The Axial Age, The Emergence of Transcendental Visions and the Rise of Clerics', *European Journal of Sociology*, 25, 1982, pp. 294–314. See also 'The Failure of Socialism', in this book, chapter 5.

39. E. A. Tiryakin, 'Puritan America in the Modern World: Mission Impossible?' Durham, unpublished manuscript, 1982. On these themes see also the chapter on the failure of socialism in the United States, in this book, chapter 5.

Index